Yasmeena's Choice

A True Story
of War, Rape, Courage
and Survival

Jean Sasson

Jacket design by Natanya Wheeler
Book design by Judith Engracia

For additional information about Jean Sasson and her books, please visit http://www.JeanSasson.com
Blog: http://jeansasson.wordpress.com/
Facebook: http://www.facebook.com/AuthorJeanSasson
Twitter: http://twitter.com/jeansasson

Other Works by Jean Sasson

Nonfiction:

The Rape of Kuwait

Princess: A True Story of Life Behind the Veil in Saudi Arabia

Princess Sultana's Daughters
(UK Title: *Daughters of Arabia*)

Princess Sultana's Circle
(UK Title: *Desert Royal*)

Mayada, Daughter of Iraq

Love in a Torn Land: A Kurdish Woman's Story

Growing Up Bin Laden: Osama's Wife and Son Reveal their Secret World

For the Love of a Son: One Afghan Woman's Quest for her Stolen Child

American Chick in Saudi Arabia
(ebook installment of forthcoming full book)

Historical Fiction:

Ester's Child
(to be re-released 2014)

Yasmeena's Choice *is dedicated to two extraordinary*

& courageous women:

For Yasmeena, wherever you are.

For Lana, may you rest in peace.

Table of Contents

The Author Remembers

Return to Kuwait: March 13, 1991

Kuwait and Kuwaitis absorb my thoughts as I sit quietly on the Freedom Flight, the first Kuwaiti government official trip into the newly freed country of Kuwait. I'm one of the 146 guests making this journey at the invitation of the Kuwaiti government.

Seven months have passed since August 2, 1990 when the Iraqi army burst upon the Kuwaitis, occupying and annexing the small Kuwaiti nation in a matter of hours. It's been six months since I traveled to London, Cairo, Riyadh and Taif so that I could interview people caught in Kuwait on that hot August day, a fateful day that transformed the momentum of the entire region. Those personal interviews were the basis for *The Rape of Kuwait*, a book I had written on the experiences of Kuwaitis and others caught in Kuwait on the first day of the invasion. When it was published in January 1991, the book became an instant best-seller, reaching #2 on the *New York Times* bestseller list.

While *Rape* revealed the stories of Kuwaitis who survived the invasion to seek safety and sanctuary in Saudi Arabia, Egypt and England, my concentration now centers on the people who remained in Kuwait during the 208-day occupation. I have been thinking about them for a long time. From media reports and personal accounts, I've come to understand that during the occupation the Iraqi army wreaked massive misery upon the Kuwaiti civilian

9

populace, including robbery, rape, physical torture and murder. Reports verify that the country was left in ruin, with devastated infrastructure and purposefully lit oil wells.

Now I'm on my way to discover for myself the result of the occupation. My plans include seeing the condition of the country, as well as meeting personally with freedom fighters and ordinary citizens who can reveal their individual accounts of what it was like to live under a ruthless occupier.

The flight time passes slowly but finally I depart from the Freedom Flight and travel by bus into Kuwait City.

War and loss are upon me from the first moment I enter the ravaged country. Everywhere I look and everyone I meet show evidence of the recent destruction by the Iraqi military. Wrecked and burned military trucks and tanks litter the roadway. I gaze upon the charred remnants of what was once a lovely home likely filled with a happy family. Such carefree days ended months before. Blazing oil fires curl and darken against a dusky sky that hides any hint of blue. I shiver from the chilly air, realizing for the first time that burning oil fires generate a miserable damp coldness rather than sweltering heat. Every living thing in Kuwait has suffered. Birds and beasts whose feathers and fur are thick with oil struggle uselessly. Those bewildered birds can no longer fly while other miserable beasts slump with hanging heads.

Later that evening, when I check into a hotel, I quietly observe the trashed interior, wondering at the splintered doors that once provided hotel guests privacy. Those doors no longer serve their intended purpose and I must pile suitcases in the open doorway of my room for the sake of my personal security.

Two days later I conduct my first interviews. Furrowed faces of grieving parents whose freedom fighting sons were tortured before their eyes quietly express their grief. I tremble at the sight of the sad children who have lost a parent as they stand mute, desperate for someone, anyone, to erase their anguish of loss. Each has its history, carrying me with them to the terrifying days of dread and horror that they have seen, that they have felt, and that they have lived.

A few weeks into my visit to Kuwait, the Kuwaiti government leads me to a story more horrific than most, a secret story deliberately kept away from the world's media, a story centered around innocent women, and a story that settled with enormous weight upon my own heart.

And I am now about to tell that story to you.

Caution to Readers

The true story you are about to read is not for the fainthearted. However, to remain authentic to this very important story, and to go beyond the headlines and statistics to raise awareness as to what really happens to women who are held as sex slaves, it is essential to include the devastatingly honest and graphic details told to me by the kidnapped women.

To protect the identities of the women who were abducted and raped, it is necessary to change their names and to modify some identifying information.

This important story gives women who survived rape and sexual torture a chance to tell their stories to the world.

This important story gives raped and murdered women a chance to rise up from their graves and have their voices heard.

This important story gives you, the reader, a story you will carry with you for the rest of your life.

Jean Sasson

Jean Sasson with Kuwaiti baby in Riyadh, Saudi Arabia
(c) The Sasson Corporation
This photo is the property of The Sasson Corporation and is not to be duplicated or
reprinted without permission.

March 15, 1991: Photo of Jean Sasson and others invited on FREEDOM
FLIGHT from Washington, DC into Kuwait. We are waiting to go into
a house of torture.
This photo was passed to Jean Sasson in June 1991 by Kuwaiti Ambassador Saudi Nasir
Al-Sabah and the author was pressed to use them in any books she wrote about the
invasion and occupation of Kuwait.

His Highness Sheik Saud Al-Abdullah Al-Salem Al-Sabah, Crown Prince & Prime Minister greeting Jean Sasson, the author who had interviewed him for her bestselling book, *The Rape of Kuwait*. Kuwaiti Ambassador to USA Nasir Al-Sabah looks on.

A reflective Ambassador Saud Nasir Al-Sabah visits his destroyed palace in Kuwait City.

These two photos were passed to Jean Sasson in June 1991 by Kuwaiti Ambassador Saudi Nasir Al-Sabah and the author was pressed to use them in any books she wrote about the invasion and occupation of Kuwait.

Following the orders of Saddam Hussein, the Iraqi army set fire to Kuwait's oilfields as they vacated the country.
(c) The Sasson Corporation

Jean Sasson with Kuwaiti Soud A. Al-Mutawa, Banker by profession volunteering as translator & driver for author.
(c) The Sasson Corporation

15

What the Kuwaitis really thought of Saddam Hussein. The dictator's photograph riddled with bullets.

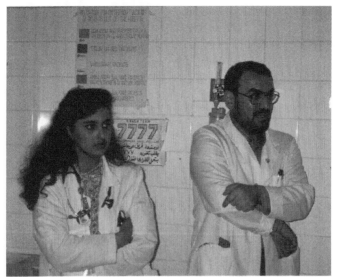

Two physicians who lived through Iraqi invasion and occupation,
telling the author the violence and horrors they personally witnessed.
(c) The Sasson Corporation

Author attended Kuwaiti celebration of those who resisted the
occupation and survived. Celebrates THE RAPE OF KUWAIT book
and photo of President George Bush.
(c) The Sasson Corporation

17

Prologue: Raped

"After victory in battle, nothing calls forth evil from its hidden den like the presence of a beautiful woman."
—Jean Sasson

There are no winners in hell. Even if you win, you lose. It's all the same. You are in hell. When Yasmeena was "chosen" by the Captain, she knew that had not won a prize. She had won a place in a man-made hell.

For many long moments she cautiously peered through the bars of her cell. She saw no one, although she heard the murmur of muffled male and female voices. Finally she turned to sit on the thin sleeping mat centered on the floor in her dimly lighted cell. She stared into nothing, her face immobile but her mind actively engaged, plotting how she might get out of hell. If she couldn't escape, she sensed that she would suffer horribly at the hands of the man who had claimed her as his own.

Yasmeena's terrifying nightmare suddenly grew more fraught when the Captain appeared to take what he said was his. He didn't glance at her as he unlocked the door to her jail cell. In fact, he appeared to be mulling other things, perhaps his family back in Iraq or a special breakfast he might prepare the following day.

The man's calm mien set off alarm bells in Yasmeena's intuition and she stood to withdraw into a corner, slowly and quietly, like a vigilant animal trainer, not wanting to arouse the attention of a beast whom the trainer knew could shift from tranquil to treacherous in an instant.

After entering the cell, the man tucked the cell key in his trouser pocket before he struggled to settle his soft and creaky body cross-legged on the thin mattress Yasmeena had vacated.

When he finally looked at her, the absence of human feeling in his eyes stirred her growing fear. He finally spoke, softly, in a dry, unemotional voice, quietly ordering, "Take off everything and let me see you."

Yasmeena stiffened. Although she was twenty-three years old, she was a virgin. She had never even kissed a man, although she had once allowed a handsome man she met in Paris to hold her hand.

The soldier's deep voice was quiet and calm, with slight hesitations softening his manner. That gentle voice seemed to make him a mild person, but Yasmeena knew that his voice was a façade. He coughed and cleared his throat, turning to spit into a corner of her cell: a man who had never been taught proper manners. Then he delivered a most alarming message in that calm voice of his. "Take off everything or I will have my men come and strip you. That will not be very pleasant for you, my dear."

Yasmeena found the power to speak although her strength faded and she could not voice louder than a whisper. "Please. Do not do this. I am an Arab. You are an Arab. I am a Muslim. You are a Muslim. Please do not do this."

He looked at her in a tranquil manner as though she had told him nothing of consequence, perhaps something as trivial as that she preferred boiled eggs to scrambled ones. His tone grew more stern when he ordered. "Take off your clothes. All of them. I want to look you over."

"Please. Think about your sister or your mother. You would not want this to happen to them. Please. Don't."

All her arguments failed to move him. He remained detached and unaffected by her fearful pleas. His impassive face was set like granite as he stood and said, "All right, then." That's when he came for her. One long step and he had her by the throat with one strong hand and with the other hand he stripped her naked, not bothering to remove her clothes delicately, but ripping them roughly off her body.

Yasmeena whimpered. All of her body felt drained and weak. She was unable to fight, but heard choking sniffles and thought for a perplexing moment that a child was in her cell until she grasped that the whimpers were coming from herself.

Then the unfeeling man pushed her to the mat and bent over her, taking a very long time to examine her body. Yasmeena prayed that he would find her lacking and would not rape her, but after many long moments of humiliation, he pronounced her "clean."

After she passed the medical test, Yasmeena watched in horror as the Captain stood up and removed his own clothes.

"Please. Please. Don't." Then she thought of a good idea, her words rushing out in a desperate appeal, "Don't. Don't. I have AIDS. I have AIDS."

Her rapist chuckled, "Arab girls don't have AIDS," he said in his maddeningly soft voice.

That's when he hurt her with his male part. Yasmeena screamed loudly but after he quietly threatened, "Stop. Scream again and I'll order every soldier under my command to enjoy you."

Yasmeena knew that this cruel man would do just that. She stifled her screams, weeping silently as she was raped repeatedly over the course of five hours.

After the assault, the Captain graciously thanked her, saying, "I had a fine time." He told her not to fret, that he would keep her for at least a month. Then, as though reciting an Arab fairy tale, he began to count off the

20

number of things that just might be in her future. And who knew what might happen in a month? He might leave Kuwait. The Kuwaitis might return. He might not kill her at the end of the month. Anything could happen.

Then he smiled a sinister smile and left her alone in a cell with only terror as an unseen companion.

Chapter One: Yasmeena

From her first moment of life, Yasmeena was gifted with beauty. Even twenty-three years after her birth, a chance encounter with a newborn would trigger animated family discussions about pretty babies. Her family agreed that Yasmeena was• the prettiest baby ever born in Lebanon.

Unlike most babies who make their first appearance red-faced with stress, the infant Yasmeena was blessed with an enviable pale ivory complexion that looked as though she spent the nine months in her mother's womb being pampered with pricey face creams. And while most babies appear annoyed over the trauma of being born, family and friends laughed gaily when remembering that the tiny Yasmeena was an instant charmer, bestowing sweet little smiles on all.

But not everyone in the family was joyful over the infant's beauty. Such a splendid baby was a cause for anxiety, according to Yasmeena's maternal grandmother, who insisted that the evil eye, or the *Isabat al'ayn*, was a real threat. Even the Prophet Muhammad said that, "The influence of an evil eye is a fact," and that "individuals have the power to cause harm from envy." While it was acceptable for admirers to welcome the newborn's safe arrival with "*Masha' Allah*" or "God has willed it," when referring to the newborn, some visitors fell so enamored of Yasmeena's beauty that they momentarily forgot that one was to never admire nor praise a baby. When thoughtless visitors complimented Yasmeena's beauty, a chorus of female voices would deny her physical appeal.

To keep Yasmeena's beauty hidden, her maternal grandmother grew enthusiastic with the baby swaddling common to infants in the region. She wound the binding to cover Yasmeena's delicate ears and draped a thin square of gauzy fabric across the baby's face in hopes of shrouding Yasmeena's uncommon beauty. Prophet Muhammad prohibited talismans to protect against the evil eye; he said only God could offer safety. But Yasmeena's grandmother conveniently forgot that restriction and attached blue ribbons, charms and buttons with seven eyes to Yasmeena's clothing. For added safety, she hung a small gold box containing a miniature Quran book over Yasmeena's cradle.

But everyone did not agree with Yasmeena's grandmother that such a beautiful baby should be concealed. Yasmeena's father was an educated, modern man and unusually proud of his first child, despite the fact she was a girl. He was delighted by his lovely daughter and demanded she be named for his favorite blossom, the Jasmine flower. Not believing in the evil eye, he crowed proudly over the beautiful child he had helped to bring into the world.

His behavior distressed and angered his watchful mother-in-law.

Female visitors hid smiles of joy to see a man so entranced with a female child, particularly since the infant was the first-born. What man in Lebanon didn't long for their first-born to be a son? Regardless of one's religious affiliation; whether Christian, Muslim or Druse, the men presented with female first-borns would be taunted by friends and intentionally insulted with the name, "father of a daughter." Those self-indulgent fathers sulked for many months, making life miserable for everyone who came near them. Truthfully, though, those mothers observing Yasmeena's unapologetic father surreptitiously wished that their own husbands would so love their own little girls.

And so the family relationships remained awkward for years. The son-in-law and the mother-in-law routinely exchanged insults, something unusual in their society where the elderly are tolerated with good humor. Yasmeena's father was a bit of a nuisance, according to his mother-in-law, who whispered her disapproval to anyone who would sit silent long enough for her to present her case. She resented her son-in-law's male meddling. What man knew anything when it came to raising babies? He even had the audacity to interrogate the women of the house each evening, insisting that they keep a written record of Yasmeena's mental and physical development.

Yasmeena's grandmother refused to enter a single Yasmeena episode in her son-in-law's ledger, bellowing in a loud voice, "My granddaughter is not a math figure to be entered into a record book!"

Certainly, no child in Lebanon was more loved than Yasmeena. When she learned to walk months earlier than the sons of his acquaintances, Yasmeena's father pronounced his daughter not only a beauty, but a genius. He forever lauded his little girl's intellect, even though Lebanese culture generally favored beauty over intelligence.

As the years passed, Yasmeena proved to be unusually perceptive and clever. Her father made plans for his daughter to assume control of his company after she obtained higher education, a novel in a country where women rarely assumed business authority over men.

No sons were born to Yasmeena's parents. As the firstborn of four daughters, Yasmeena's crown as favored child remained atop her head. As the years passed, Yasmeena's beauty continued to blossom. More significantly, her astuteness and insight grew even stronger. Mercifully, flattery never spoiled Yasmeena. She was modest and kind, so the mélange of beauty and brains did not spur female envy and animosity.

Yasmeena's father expressed only one criticism of his lovely child. Yasmeena was so sensitive to others that he fretted her compassion would bring many problems. He believed that his daughter should instead develop the stern demeanor so admired in the male children of his business acquaintances. But Yasmeena couldn't control her sympathetic nature. When she witnessed any injustice, she stepped forward to protect the less fortunate, even if it meant that she had to lash out at male children, something Lebanese girls were taught never to do.

Other idiosyncrasies arose when Yasmeena matured into a teenager. She startled her parents, sisters and friends when she announced she was not enticed by the idea of early marriage, a practice common in Lebanese Muslim culture. Yasmeena went even further when she confided to her best friend, Nadia, that she did not share her dreams of becoming a young wife and mother. In fact, she was beginning to notice that marriage equaled little more than being a servant to a man and to his children.

Nadia was clearly aghast while listening to the strong-minded Yasmeena explain that marriage was favorable to men and detrimental to women. "Nadia, listen to me, cooking three meals a day, supervising servants to maintain a clean villa, and keeping a contented husband brings on premature aging. Look around at our friends who are still in their twenties," Yasmeena grumbled. "After the birth of only two children, most appear much older than their years!"

The truth was that Yasmeena secretly enjoyed her beauty and knew that her looks opened doors of opportunity. In fact, she hoped that her beauty might help to get her out of the small country of Lebanon so that she could travel the world.

Knowing that her parents would not approve, she kept her silence when she applied for the job of airline hostess with a major Middle Eastern airliner with offices

25

in Beirut. She was offered the position during that first interview. From the manner of the male supervisor's conduct, Yasmeena understood that her striking looks and good figure drove his decision. Airlines in the Middle East were behind modern ideas when it came to women's liberation, and suffered no regulations that forced companies to regard age or weight discrimination when hiring women. In fact, the airlines laid little emphasis on higher education or academic achievement, chiefly hiring young female hostesses solely to enhance the beauty of the plush interiors of their planes, like expensive decorations that could walk and talk.

In the beginning, Yasmeena's father was disappointed that his daughter spurned the opportunity to earn her university degree at any college she chose. But he was so enamored of his sweet Yasmeena that he quickly rationalized her decision by declaring, "Really, it is beneficial for a woman to travel and to gain a little experience before assuming control of a large company." He also quietly approved her postponing marriage, as he felt that no man was truly worthy of his daughter. Yasmeena's mother mainly fretted that her daughter would harm her reputation by traveling the world without male protection. But even her mother soon calmed after she questioned her younger daughters to discover that Yasmeena had confided she had never dated, and probably would not. When Yasmeena was ready for marriage, she would come home and ask her parents to arrange a good match. Both her father and mother were reassured as they saw that, when not traveling for her new job, their liberated daughter continued to live in the family home and seemed the same Yasmeena she always had been: modest, neat and sweet.

And so Yasmeena embraced the independent life, so joyful upon her first visit to Paris that she wandered the beautiful city streets for days with an impish smile lighting her face. Her dreams were coming true. She was happier still when she reflected on her nineteen-year-old sister in Beirut, whose life was a mirror of what Yasmeena had avoided. Her sister's first child was due any day. Her belly was so large that she waddled like a duck. Although her sister claimed to be ecstatic over an early marriage to a successful businessman, sometimes her protests of happiness seemed thin, particularly when she confided to her mother and Yasmeena that her husband demanded sex at all hours of the day or night, regardless of how her first pregnancy exhausted her. Sex with her husband was the last thing on her mind. She was expected to cater to his every desire. Yasmeena's mother had little sympathy for her daughter, advising that it was her duty to keep her husband contented both in and out of the bedroom.

But Yasmeena had felt enormous pity for her little sister's situation since that day. Now she often observed her sister's weary expression while waiting on her husband. Like most Lebanese sons, her husband had been wholly spoiled by his mother and now he kept his wife busy demanding one thing or another to be placed in his hands, as if he were a child.

Just thinking about the grinding life her sister was leading sometimes caused Yasmeena to whoop with joy that she had escaped such an existence.

Invasion of Kuwait:
Iraqi troops cross the Kuwait border today and penetrated deeply into Kuwait's capital city...As blasts shook the capital, Kuwait radio appealed for citizens to help repel the attack, Reuters said. "Your country is being subjected to a barbaric invasion." Kuwait radio went on to say, "It is time to defend it."
—*The New York Times* (World)
August 2, 1990

Iraqis Exult, A Bit Warily
Motorists honked their horns and flashed their lights here
today to celebrate the Iraqi Army's invasion of Kuwait.
—*Reuters* in Baghdad, Iraq
August 2, 1990

In the summer of 1990, Kuwait had an estimated
population of 2,155,000. More than 60% of the population
was non-Kuwaiti and were mainly foreign workers. At the
time of the invasion, it is thought that at least one third of
the native Kuwaiti population was vacationing abroad
while the remainder were in the country, although during
the seven month occupation, many other Kuwaitis fled
into Saudi Arabia and from there travelled to London or
other European capitals where they waited for their
country to be freed.
—Estimated Figures from Kuwaiti Embassy
Washington, D.C.
August 1990

    While Yasmeena enjoyed a few years of the
independent working girl's life, her days of carefree
happiness came to an abrupt end on August 2, 1990.
    After working as an airline hostess for two years,
Yasmeena had built a network of friendships. She often
switched work days with girlfriends in her same position.
So it was a routine request when a friend who wanted
early leave for holiday asked Yasmeena to work the
Kuwait City flight on Wednesday, August 1, 1990. The
flight arrived on schedule that Wednesday afternoon and
the tired crew travelled into Kuwait City for their
scheduled layover. They were slated to depart the

following afternoon on Thursday, August 2, 1990 to return to Dubai and from there on to Beirut.

After eating a club sandwich and cup of soup in the hotel restaurant, Yasmeena kept to her usual routine and retired early. She was sleeping soundly when loud blasts woke her. She first believed it was a wedding celebration at the hotel, but when she opened her eyes to check the time, she was mystified to see that it was nearly 3 a.m. Hotels in Kuwait rarely allowed festivities to go past 1 a.m.

Yasmeena turned on her side and pulled a pillow over her head. But sleep was impossible because the commotion grew louder. She sighed as she got out of bed to peer from her hotel window. Shocked to see armed soldiers running in the streets, she rubbed her eyes and looked again. Yes, there they were, a bunch of men moving from one building to another, shooting at each other. Red and white blasts flared against the dark night sky. She rubbed her eyes again. The setting looked like an action scene from a Hollywood movie. But there were no movies being filmed in Kuwait City.

Yasmeena stumbled backward to sit on the edge of her bed and think. Was this a government coup? Was the Al-Sabah royal family being overthrown? For sure, the Kuwaiti press exercised one of the most uninhibited voices in the Middle East. Some journalists had been airing complaints for months, urging Kuwait to move from a monarchy to a democracy. She then had a hazy memory of growing problems between Iraq and Kuwait and wondered if Saddam's armies had invaded. Surely not. After fighting Iran for eight long years, why would the Iraqi dictator start a second war with yet another neighbor?

She returned to peek from behind the curtains again, but could not see clearly enough to know exactly who was involved in the battle. Her heart pounded because she had a keen respect for war and violence. She had been born during Lebanon's civil war, and despite her youth, she could recall the savagery of that conflict. Lebanon's war grew so fierce that for several years her family lived in neighboring Cyprus. Her family was lucky then: No one in their immediate family had been killed, and most of their properties had survived. Only a few of her father's warehouses were destroyed when the Maronites fired rockets at the Shiite community directly behind those buildings. Now her father's business was prospering once again.

When the battle noises outside her window grew louder, Yasmeena knew that she had to do something. She opened her suitcase and pulled out a blouse and skirt. She quickly removed her nightgown, the pretty blue one with an image of the Eiffel Tower, and rapidly dressed. That's when she heard excited guests running in the hallway. She joined them.

In the lobby she saw several of her colleagues and connected with them, huddling together nervously waiting for news. The hotel management soon sent employees around the hotel to announce to shocked guests that the Iraqi military had invaded Kuwait. After only a few hours, guests were told, the small country was overrun and everyone was trapped.

Yasmeena and her colleagues were so stunned by their new reality that they couldn't decide what to do; so they did nothing. Finally Yasmeena suggested that they eat breakfast while they had the opportunity. Who knew what might happen? "It will be better to have a full stomach if we are taken to jail," she said with a merry laugh, as though jail was a ridiculous idea.

After eating a modest breakfast they returned as a group to their supervisor's hotel room where they sat for a while, trying to make international calls on his room telephone to alert their families that they were unharmed, but phone service no longer worked. Eventually the group wandered back to the restaurant and nibbled on a light lunch. Just as they were being served tea and dessert, Iraqi soldiers burst into the hotel. The agitated soldiers made a deafening uproar as they raced through the narrow hallways, knocking down guest room doors with their feet or with their heavy weapons.

Frightened hotel guests listened in disbelief when the fierce-faced men pointed weapons and shouted that they were confiscating the hotel for the convenience of Iraqi soldiers. "Everyone outside!" they ordered.

Thankfully she had not fully unpacked her bag the night before, so Yasmeena took a chance to dash to her room. She escaped with her belongings and gathered with her colleagues on the grassy area outside the hotel. There they all talked at once, trying to determine the best course of action. The flight crew supervisor suggested that the Iraqis had invaded only to force the Kuwaiti royal family to give Saddam some of Kuwait's wealth. "Once the Al-Sabah family pays the bribe," he said with authority, "Saddam will pull his soldiers back."

Yasmeena said nothing but recalled how stubborn Saddam had been during his eight-year battle with Iran. He was not a man who gave up anything easily.

Yasmeena's thoughts became increasingly distracted because the road noise was deafening. Kuwaitis sped along the normally peaceful residential street, dashing home to get to their families, Yasmeena assumed. She remembered a Beirut talk show she had seen a few weeks earlier in which the host bemoaned Beirut traffic and predicted that soon cars would be able to lift off highways and fly like helicopters.

Yasmeena yearned that one of those flying cars appear so she flee Kuwait and return to Lebanon. Just as she was daydreaming about helicopter rescue, the father of one of Yasmeena's Kuwaiti girlfriends happened to drive to the front of the hotel. He recognized Yasmeena in the crowd of guests and stopped his car, leaning his head through the window to tell her, "Yasmeena, have you heard the news? The Iraqis are here. Come; come and stay with my family until this is sorted out."

Yasmeena wished he would invite all her friends to go with her, but knew that it was too much to ask this man to assume responsibility for twelve people. So a relieved Yasmeena told her supervisor, "I will go. Then you don't have to find accommodation for me. I'll meet up with you when the airport reopens."

Her supervisor agreed, "Yes, that's best. We will see you at the airport."

Yasmeena threw her small case into the automobile and climbed into the back seat. She believed that she would be safer living with a prominent Kuwaiti family. She knew that her colleagues would have to rely on strangers to help them.

Yasmeena settled in gratefully at her Kuwaiti girlfriend's home. She felt safe, at first. After only a few days, Kuwait appeared to be fully subjugated, though Iraqis had not yet laid down new laws. During that time, most people did not feel personal physical danger. But the Iraqi soldiers soon grasped the levers of control and began to pluck all the riches they found in shops and Kuwaiti private homes. They were enthusiastic thieves, appropriating everything of value: jewelry, gold watches, televisions and fancy furniture.

Yasmeena and her girlfriend watched in horror when boisterous soldiers came to their neighborhood, stealing anything they could carry or load to their military trucks. After they took all the money, jewelry, televisions and posh furnishings, those rowdy soldiers began to grab beloved pets, many of them expensive breeds, stuffing terrified cats, howling dogs and exotic birds into cans or boxes, shouting to anyone who would listen that they would sell those pricey pets for a big fee in the Baghdad souks.

The soldiers' motivation to steal was easy to trace. After Iraq's long war with Iran, nearly all Iraqis other than Saddam's family and his tribal cousins were impoverished. Saddam's brutish regime had left the poor even poorer than before.

In Kuwait, never had ordinary Iraqi soldiers seen such wealth. Some of the excited soldiers were walking around with four or five gold Rolexes clasped to their wrists.

Yasmeena yearned for them to leave so that she could return to Beirut to her worried parents. Perhaps, she hoped, when Saddam's soldiers emptied Kuwait of everything valuable they would go back to Baghdad where they belonged.

Chapter Two: Captured!

Iraq Remaps Kuwait as Province 19:
Baghdad, Iraq – This nation redrew the world map Tuesday, erasing Kuwait from the face of the globe and making the former emirate its new, and clearly its richest, southernmost province. In a decree from President Saddam Hussein, Iraq spared no effort in removing every reference to the name of the nation that was its southern neighbor for more than a century, officially designating Kuwait as Province 19. The same decree ordered that the nation's capital of Kuwait City will now be known as the provincial capital of Kadhima, an ancient Arabic name for the region.
—*Los Angeles Times*
August 29, 1990

Kuwaitis stumbled in shock for the first few weeks of the Iraqi occupation. The Kuwaiti government had fled the country on the first day of the invasion. They were now operating out of the mountain city of Taif, Saudi Arabia. The Kuwaiti military had been quickly overrun. Civilians were left to deal with an aggressive Iraqi army with no good deeds in their minds.

By nature, Kuwaitis were not a war-minded people. Those left to contend with the Iraqi military were mainly civilians of a small rich nation who had never in their lives known violence. The ordinary Kuwaiti citizen minded his own business, accumulated wealth, and didn't think much about the routine disorder that too often visited the rest of the Arab world. At least that was Yasmeena's opinion.

After the invasion, though, everything changed. The Kuwaitis, whom Yasmeena had once considered soft from so much wealth, soon proved to Yasmeena that the gentleness cloaked men of resolve and strength. Kuwaiti men rose up like angry lions to defend their country.

Yasmeena methodically noted the activities of the family that had offered her sanctuary. She soon recognized that the members were of one mind and that they would struggle against the invaders in any way possible. The two sons, both in their twenties, were deeply involved in the new Kuwaiti underground. The men bravely contested the Iraqi fighters, even after the Kuwaiti military was overpowered.

As for the Iraqi soldiers, they appeared stupefied to discover that Kuwaitis had no desire to be made a part of Iraq. Kuwait City was renamed Kadhima and declared the 19th province of Iraq, but the Kuwaitis rebuffed the claim and organized a hardy resistance. But Kuwaiti tenacity against foreign rule triggered a fiercer counteraction from the Iraqi soldiers.

Before long, the Iraqis assumed that all young Kuwaiti men were a part of the resistance, and targeted all Kuwaiti men of a certain age. When free travel in the country became difficult for the Kuwaiti men, the men tapped their sisters or cousins to transport weapons and important documents. For a time, the Iraqis didn't suspect women as resistance fighters, so the plan initially met with great success, at least in the beginning.

Although the nighttime belonged to the Kuwaiti resistance, Kuwait's cities were calm during daylight hours. In monotony of the tedious days, jaded Iraqi soldiers sought distraction. There was little entertainment available because the entire country had been gutted, including the amusement parks, which were now stacked in colorful metal piles all around Baghdad.

35

The Iraqi soldiers imagined perhaps that the "silent Kuwaitis" who had not yet joined the resistance might issue invitations for dinner or parties. But they were wrong. Although some Palestinians and various other nationalities working in the kingdom cooperated with the Iraqis, Kuwaitis scorned the invaders. The bored Iraqis were easily offended, developing quick-trigger tempers that erupted when Kuwaitis spurned their offers of friendship.

As the days passed, the Iraqi soldiers grew even nastier. Far from home, they did what so many soldiers of war have done since the beginning of human civilization: They began raping women.

From Kuwaiti neighbors, Yasmeena heard whispers that Iraqi soldiers were attacking women in their homes. Yasmeena and the other women of the household listened anxiously when it was reported that the soldiers had established a routine. They would break down doors, truss the men with ropes and secure them in separate areas. Then they would force the women to strip and would take turns raping any and all females from the ages of twelve to forty...or even fifty if the older woman had maintained a youthful appearance.

Other accounts reported that soldiers sometimes eyed the women at established roadblocks. If the soldiers found any of the female passengers physically desirable, they would hold the Kuwaiti men at gunpoint and quickly take the women away to be raped.

Several gun battles broke out at roadblocks when armed Kuwaiti men defended their women.

Due to these stories, the women of the household didn't protest when the men of the house told them to hide if they heard unknown male voices.

"After Iraq's invasion, Kuwaitis are being subjected to looting, rape, torture, and executions. Based on scores of interviews with refugees, we have found a horrifying picture of widespread arrests, torture under interrogation, summary executions, mass rapes, and extrajudicial killings."
—*Amnesty International*
September 1990

But after a few weeks, talk of sexual attacks diminished. Everyone believed that the worst had passed when they heard the erroneous report that Baghdad had ordered such lawlessness to cease. The truth was that Iraqi soldiers had recently devised a different scheme to seize females to rape.

After living a few weeks with her Kuwaiti hosts, one of the sons of the household asked Yasmeena if she would consider driving a bundle of leaflets to a different section of the city. She agreed, instantly eager to support the family that had welcomed her into their home. She knew that the resistance was growing more powerful, and that the Iraqis were on heightened alert for hidden weapons and other resistance materials, but at the time she believed that their focus was still solely on men. Just the day before, Yasmeena and her Kuwaiti friend had driven through a roadblock at which the Iraqi soldiers merely smiled and waved.

While getting dressed for the assignment, Yasmeena was excited. She was finally going to do something worthwhile.

Several hours later, Yasmeena was happy to be driving alone, feeling almost normal, free and happy. She was humming along to the memorable tune *"Ya Habayeb,"* or *"My Loved Ones,"* by Najwa Karam, an-up-and coming Lebanese singing star. Music had always lifted Yasmeena's spirits and today was no different. Also, she was pleased to help her friends in the important cause of resistance.

She had no way of knowing that on that very day, Iraqi soldiers were implementing a new order from Baghdad. The Iraqi command in Kuwait had been told that all adults living in Kuwait, regardless of their nationality, sex or age, were now suspected of criminal behavior. All were to be halted and their vehicles searched. There were to be no exceptions.

Ignorant of the new orders, Yasmeena confidently went on her way. She felt no danger. She was familiar with most of the roadblocks in the area, and she had her documents ready to show, although she doubted she would need them.

Her mood changed quickly when she arrived at the first roadblock on Athilali Street, which was one of the most important streets in the capital. She smiled at the young soldier who stood by her window. The soldier did not return her smile. Unmoved by her youth and beauty, his expression was unwavering as he regarded her in a cold, brisk manner. After staring impersonally at her for a few moments, he demanded that she step out of, and away from, the vehicle while they conducted their search.

Everything quickly fell apart. Three soldiers attacked the automobile as though it were their dedicated enemy. They ripped apart the seat leather with a sharp instrument. They worked like robots, moving on to examine the underside of the automobile with a mirror attached to a long reed-like stick. They then lifted the hood, examining the engine as though they had never seen one before.

Yasmeena was numb with fear, for she knew that the brothers had hidden the flyers in the trunk of the automobile. Those flyers were tucked into the backs of ten large picture frames, each depicting a London landmark. Other items were scattered in the trunk, put there to divert the attention of any soldier conducting a search.

There were several dolls and stuffed animals, all of which were quickly ripped to bits with a sharp knife. There was a bag of women's clothing, which was examined before being brusquely tossed to the side of the road. The soldiers at first dismissed the picture frames, until one sharp-eyed soldier noticed that the frames were without glass, and that the London photographs bulged from the frames.

Yasmeena gasped for air when the soldier tore open the frame and flyers showered out. Yasmeena stared helplessly at the floating debris, whispering to herself, "I am doomed. I am doomed. God help me, I am doomed."

Despite her fear, she kept her composure while showing the soldiers her Lebanese identity papers. "I am not even Kuwaiti," she said. "I have no fight with you Iraqis. Why would I break any laws?" She gestured at the automobile. "Just yesterday I found this car. It had keys in the ignition. It was left with the doors open. I waited for an hour and no one claimed it." She gazed meaningfully at the oldest of the men, the one with the most medals on his uniform, telling him, "You know that many foolish Kuwaitis are discarding their automobiles. I took an abandoned car. I have not even looked into the trunk of this car, believe me."

The older soldier gave her a shrewd look, trying to decide if she was telling the truth. He knew that what Yasmeena said about the Kuwaitis and their automobiles was accurate. Soon after invading the country, the Iraqis announced that Kuwait no longer existed. All Kuwaiti documents and registrations were no longer valid. All Kuwaiti vehicle registrations were invalid. Everyone must register as an Iraqi because there was no such thing as a Kuwaiti. According to the Iraqis, Kuwaitis had vanished from the earth, just like the dinosaurs.

But Kuwaitis were outraged by the order. They were Kuwaiti and proud of it. They would not so easily discard their Kuwaiti identification papers and registrations. Rather than submit to Iraqi orders, they hid their automobiles, determined not to drive them until the Iraqis were driven from their country. If they were driving their automobiles and saw an unexpected roadblock ahead, they stopped and abandoned their vehicles and walked, instead. Some Kuwaitis burned their expensive vehicles, saying they preferred to do so than submit to Iraqi orders. It would be good for their health to take up walking, they agreed.

Soon the Iraqi soldiers realized that the ordinary Kuwaiti was bolder than the average Iraqi. Long ago Saddam had beaten the spirit out of the Iraqis. Of course, this happened after Iraqis learned the hard way how Saddam Hussein responded to disobedience.

The Kuwaitis still had a lot of spirit and plenty of pride.

Yasmeena was not worried that her exposure would endanger her Kuwaiti hosts. The automobile could not be traced to the family. She knew that the resistance employed automobiles abandoned by fleeing Palestinians or Indians or other nationalities so that the vehicle could not be tracked back to any Kuwaiti family still living in the country.

Yasmeena felt a brief flicker of hope. Perhaps the soldiers would believe her lie that she had found the automobile and decided to take it. How could she know that the resistance had stuffed some of their flyers in the picture frames? She knew that there was no date stamped on the flyers so the timeliness of her travel could not be gauged.

The old soldier could not make up his mind. Had the moment not been so grave, Yasmeena would have seen the humor in his indecision. He pursed his lips and sighed and stared at Yasmeena, then his eyes crossed two or three times, for what reason she did not know. But caution overcame his desire to release her, for finally he motioned for Yasmeena to be handcuffed. She was then pushed into a military vehicle where she sat and listened to four soldiers discuss where to take her.

The soldiers briefly debated before one of the younger men determined her future. Rather than deliver her to the prison especially for resistance members, the soldier said that he knew of a special prison suitable for her. After a long pause, the old soldier agreed for him to take her. Yasmeena stared at the man, her eyes pleading, but the old soldier turned away to question another driver.

Yasmeena's fate was set from that moment. She was too numb to protest further when the soldier ordered her to move from that vehicle and follow him to another. Yasmeena was thinking, remembering that she had recently heard that Kuwaiti men discovered transporting items for the rebellion were always tortured before being executed. Was she being taken to be tortured and executed?

Never had she felt so helpless. Rescue would be impossible because no one had any idea what was happening to her.

She was relieved not to be blindfolded and thus observed everything around her. Her thoughts were whirling, her mind moving as fast as a spinning propeller. Perhaps she would get an opportunity to escape and if she did, she wanted to know which direction to run. Soon the soldier turned into a side street and drove to an unfamiliar area of the city. By this time, Yasmeena was certain that she was being taken for torture and execution. Or perhaps they executed prisoners on the outskirts of the city, perhaps in the desert? But before they left the city, the soldier stopped at a squat, nondescript beige building that was clearly a neighborhood prison.

Ordered to leave the vehicle and go into the prison, Yasmeena did as she was told. As she was walking toward the prison entrance, two Iraqi soldiers were leaving. It took her a confused moment to realize that the two men were pulling a young Arab woman by her hair. The girl was weeping.

Yasmeena gasped. Weakness went through her entire body until her legs sagged like soft wax, making it nearly impossible to stand. She paused, trying to gather her strength as she attempted to learn what was going on with the young woman. Her guard shouted at her and pushed her into the building. Quickly she heard a barrage of gunshots and knew that she was being taken to a prison where executions did occur.

At that realization she yearned that her arms might sprout propellers so that she might soar over the building and fly like a bird with powerful wings away from those sounds of death, but her all-too-human body grounded her.

Her unsmiling guard warned her that girls who did not cooperate were eliminated. That menacing man used his finger to slice across his own neck. A second guard appeared. He looked at Yasmeena and grinned, then hissed like a cobra, bringing to mind the shocking time a real cobra snake carelessly handled at a street fair in Bombay was flashed near to her face. As the snake passed inches away, its head got even larger and its cavernous mouth opened wide and it hissed loudly. Yasmeena had nearly fainted at the sight. Now the hissing man caused a similar shock. She stood without moving until an unseen hand pushed her into an empty cell. A gravelly voiced man curtly ordered to stand to attention, "Don't move!"

There she stood with her brown eyes shining with tears, her hair gleaming, and her face frozen in panic. A dozen men walked back and forth, all looking at her with alert eyes, their heads moving like automated robots, scanning every inch of her from head to toe, with protruding eyes lingering longest on her chest area.

For the first time in her life her breasts felt like enemies who imperiled her life. Yasmeena resembled her mother, who had large breasts and now those inherited

42

breasts were prompting grown men to scheme what they might do if they could clutch them in their hands or use them as a pillow for their faces. The scene of eager men plotting assault on her body was like watching a perverted movie. She could barely think, although her head pounded with the knowledge that she was in the worst predicament of her life.

Then a muted but deep voice was heard and the men quieted. A tall Iraqi with a look of stern command suddenly loomed before her, his unexpressive gaze so unlike the other men. After a few moments, he nodded and said, "This one is mine." The other men scattered, their interest vanishing for a woman they knew that they would never possess. Their Captain had spoken.

The man they called Captain meandered down the long hallway, leaving Yasmeena's vision without once speaking directly to her.

Chapter Three: Sex Slave

Ten hours after being humiliated and continually raped, Yasmeena sat motionless, staring but not seeing, her body covered with a dirty brown blanket. Physically numb from the pain of the assault, she dared not move. Her entire body throbbed in pain, but nowhere more than her private area. Blood had flowed from down there for a long time after the captain left her, and now she was fearful that blood might once again gush, so she sat very still. Although soldiers walked past her, their leering stares confirmed that they were indifferent to her plight. This prison was ruled by men whose hearts were made of stone and none would offer assistance or escape.

Yasmeena was terribly disturbed that it was a Muslim man who had raped her. Muslim men were supposed to protect Muslim women, or so she had been taught from childhood. Like most Muslim women, since the moment of her birth Yasmeena had lived in a bubble of protection. She knew little of men and their sexual appetites because she was kept at a distance from sexual matters, a topic prohibited to unmarried women. Prior to seeking a career as an air hostess, she had rarely ventured outside her family circle. Even after she began to travel for work, her fellow stewardesses watched out for each other. Yasmeena was seldom alone.

Now she was truly alone for the first time in her life. But it would be a brief respite, as she soon saw her rapist make his way toward her cell.

She flinched when she saw that his expression was aloof. From her earlier experience she knew that the evil

44

in his mind was not visible in his eyes or facial expression. But clearly he was now on a mission. With one hand he carried an electronic device and in the other he balanced a chair. He was a clumsy man, and after unlocking her jail cell, he stumbled around, banging the chair against the metal bars, then putting the chair in a corner of her small cell. He placed the radio/recording device on the floor before dragging a small wooden stool from the corner, a stool that Yasmeena had not noticed until that moment. He settled into the chair and propped his feet on the stool. He huffed from his labors but his attitude remained understated. Like the evening before, he was a man unmoved by his evil act of raping a virginal woman. He stared at her for many long moments before asking, "Did you have a good time last night?"

Yasmeena gulped, but didn't answer.

He smirked, "I know you had a good time. You might as well admit it."

Yasmeena sat silently but trembled in fear, waiting for a second sexual assault from this man she did not know.

He asked, "Do you need anything?" before glancing around the cell taking inventory, Yasmeena assumed.

Her mouth was so dry that she found it difficult to speak, finally speaking two important words, "Food. Water."

The rapist looked surprised, realizing for the first time that she had been left for many hours without any water or nourishment. He called out to his men, ordering them to bring food, water and two buckets, one for washing and the other to use as a toilet.

"My men will supply you," he said. "Eat something. Take a bath." He stood up. "I will be back." He smiled his creepy smile once more. "We will have some real fun afterward. It will be even better than last night."

45

Although Yasmeena was sick to her stomach from dread of what she must endure, she choked down a few bites of an unsalted boiled egg and a piece of stale pita bread. She drank a glass of lukewarm apple juice before relieving herself in the bucket. She made an attempt to wash her body, but was so sore that she found it difficult to do little more than pat herself with a damp cloth.

The Captain kept his promise to return. He sat for a while, acting as though he was there for a pleasant visit and speaking quietly about the most mundane things, even complaining about the difficulty of finding a good laundry in Kuwait City to have his uniform cleaned. He was irritated because laundry workers had fled the country.

Yasmeena, still stunned from the trauma of being raped, sat without speaking, forcing herself to display interest in his words, wondering if the Captain was trying to convince himself that his depravity was normal.

Too soon he was ready for "fun," as he called it, and once again he ordered Yasmeena to undress. He told her of his plans as she slowly pulled off her ripped shirt and slipped out of her torn skirt. He said, "I watched an American movie this morning. I want you to do something special that I saw."

Yasmeena's body was shaking so hard that her teeth clattered.

Her rapist moved the chair behind an extended wall that hid a small corner of the cell. Yasmeena assumed the wall was there to provide privacy for prisoners to use the toilet pot or to bathe.

The Captain was very specific when telling her what she must do. He explained the radio/tape device, "I brought a music tape especially for us. The music will play. While the music is playing you will do what I tell you to do."

Yasmeena soon understood that she was supposed to perform like a stripper, something she knew nothing about. She stood shaking and naked, although her hands instinctively covered her private parts. She burst into tears. "I cannot. I cannot. I don't know what you want," she protested.

He pursed his lips. "You will please me, or you will please every soldier under my command. The choice is yours, my dear."

She nodded but did not speak, too dazed by the idea that she must accept one form of torture to avoid an even greater torture. She would be raped by one man or by dozens of men. That's when realization fully hit her. She must please her rapist or she would be forced to endure rapes by many men.

The Captain quickly stripped off his own clothes and sat in the chair.

She studiously avoided looking at his body.

He flipped a switch on the tape recorder and the music began. Motioning for her to climb on top of him, he grunted, "Do as I told you."

Yasmeena felt her body was as inflexible as the wooden chair, but remembering his threat to order his men to rape her, she tried unsuccessfully to repeat what he had exhibited to her. She could not bear to see his eager face anticipating her body so she closed her eyes. She felt her heavy breasts swaying and was more humiliated than any woman could ever be. She was a complete failure as a dancer because she tried to keep her nude body as far away from her rapist as possible. The Captain began to groan, indicating that he wanted everything again, so he forcefully pulled her down and raped her yet again.

Still sore from the night before, she began to weep but her tears provoked him to rape her even more vigorously.

Time passed slowly. Perhaps two hours later, he finally left. He departed in a good mood, promising to return soon. Before he left he stroked one of her breasts and said, "That was the best.

As Yasmeena lay exhausted and naked on the floor, tears streamed from her eyes and across her cheeks and into her ears. Just when she thought nothing in life could be worse, she heard the most anguished cries she had ever heard. The screeches she was hearing were even louder than the time when her younger sister had stuck her hand into a boiling pot of water and was burned so seriously that she was taken to the hospital.

What was happening? Was a girl being tortured to death?

The unlucky girl screamed until Yasmeena put her index fingers into her ears, trying without success to shut out the agony.

The following day the Captain informed Yasmeena that she was one of fifteen girls being kept in the prison. All were there to service the soldiers. "We deserve it," he said. "We are soldiers who risk our lives. Our wives and girlfriends are not available to us. It is understood that we need women or we will be unable to perform our duties as soldiers. If men do not have women, they will become too weak to fight. This is known by all people with intelligence."

Yasmeena ignored his ignorant talk but built her courage to ask, "Who was that girl screaming? She screamed for more than an hour."

The Captain had a blank look on his face for a few seconds then said, "Oh. That girl. She's a Kuwaiti girl. Her name is Lana or something like that. She's not very clever. She keeps fighting to hold on to something that has already been lost." He grinned, considering himself a comedian, Yasmeena assumed.

She spoke without thinking. "Can I visit her?"

48

To her surprise the Captain stared at her without speaking, then shrugged. "Why not. You are a smart girl. Perhaps you can convince her to cooperate. Her noisy struggles are disturbing me. If she does not stop her unruliness, I will order her shot."

A chill ran through Yasmeena's body. Her rapist was so convinced of the men's right to kidnap and rape women that he was angered when a victim didn't embrace her rapist. At that moment Yasmeena knew that she must be submissive or he would give the order for her to be shot, too. At the same time she was cooperating, she would try to outwit him. Meanwhile, she would be a compliant woman who accepted his sexual attacks.

And so when he reached out for her body she forced herself to sit still, to accept what was coming. He yanked at her dress, pulling it down to her waist, roughly grabbing her breasts. She watched in revulsion as his rubbery lips opened and his tongue explored her body. She forgot her decision to cooperate and instinctively pulled away, but his eyes glinted in anger and for the first time he showed his violent side. Without a word of warning his mouth opened wide and he bit down hard, twice on both breasts, before chewing on them then like he was famished and dinner had been served. Something told Yasmeena that she was at a dangerous crossroads with the Captain, so she gulped hard and accepted his bites, even forcing a smile as though she had been waiting for her entire life for this man to chew on her breasts.

The Captain kept chewing and she kept smiling. Yasmeena fearfully envisioned the man consuming her entire body, swallowing her flesh one tiny bite after another. But he didn't.

Chapter Four: Lana

Two days later Yasmeena was startled when one of the guards came to her cell. He said that he was to escort her to visit with one of the prisoners. Yasmeena grew instantly excited. Since being kidnapped, her conversation had been limited solely to the man who was brutally raping her. She now knew that her rapist was going to keep his promise and allow her to visit with the Kuwaiti girl.

Earlier in the morning Yasmeena had taken a sponge bath and was dressed in a fancy cloak the Captain had ordered her to wear, so she was instantly ready to walk out of her claustrophobia cell.

The guard escort curtly ordered Yasmeena, "Do not look." So she did as she was told, knowing that she must be obedient or her Captain would refuse all future requests. She stared straight ahead without lingering to look at any other prisoners, although she was eager to meet all of the women, to hear their stories, and most importantly, to comfort and receive comfort in turn. She knew that all the captive women might gain strength if they could only say a few words to the other. But that was not to be, at least not yet.

After passing a few cells, her guard stopped in front of a particular barred cell door. Yasmeena eagerly peered into the cell, wanting to finally meet the Lana whose screams she had heard previously. She could see only that someone small was sleeping on a mat, her entire body hidden under a soiled blanket. This must be the girl Lana, Yasmeena decided.

Yasmeena was soon locked in the cell with the sleeping prisoner, and the guard intoned, "I will be back in one hour."

There was no movement under the blanket. Yasmeena hoped that the girl was not dead. Her heartrending screams during the previous night had convinced Yasmeena that she was being murdered. There was no mistaking Lana's screams for any of the other girl's pleas. Lana's frenzied terror was in a category all to itself.

Yasmeena spoke softly, "Lana? I am Yasmeena. I am here for a visit."

There was no movement.

"Lana?"

The blanket pushed aside and a small, delicate face appeared. The girl said nothing, but she blinked, clearly disconcerted by the sight of an unexpected visitor.

"It is all right, Lana. I have permission to visit."

Lana blinked again. Although Lana was in need of a bath, the grime that had accumulated on her face did nothing to diminish her beauty. Yasmeena straightaway determined that Lana was the most beautiful female she had ever seen. Every feature of her face was perfection. Her large dark eyes were almond-shaped and brimming with expression. Dramatic black eyebrows resembled perfect wings. Her nose was delicate and her pink lips full. The girl had light-colored skin and silky black hair. If she lived in America, someone would entice her to Hollywood where she would become a movie star, perhaps competing for the coveted title of the most beautiful girl in the world.

Yasmeena stood quietly without speaking. Lana was so beautiful that it would require an effort to shift one's eyes from her face. Yasmeena felt herself plain in comparison, although she knew that most people found her very attractive.

"Who are you?" Lana asked in a quiet but hoarse voice.

"I am Yasmeena. I am a prisoner, too. The Captain claimed me."

"Oh," Lana murmured sorrowfully, "Be careful. Be careful. That Captain already kidnapped two Kuwaiti girls. After only a few days, he had them both executed."

Yasmeena blanched, but regained her composure. She was not surprised. She had already surmised that her rapist was a dangerous man. That calm face and soft voice veiled a wall of hostility. After only a week of being raped by the Captain, she could imagine that he had raped other girls with a coldness that would enable him to order their executions after only a few days of raping.

"You are right, Lana. All must be very cautious in this place."

Yasmeena sat down, telling Lana something of her ill-fated journey to the prison. Lana listened, happy to have someone near other than her brutal rapist.

At the end of her personal tale of grief, Yasmeena asked, "What about you, Lana? How did you come to be in this place?

Lana sighed. "I should be in London today. I should not have been in Kuwait City on the day the Iraqis invaded. But my youngest sister had taken ill the week before, on the very day that our family was to leave on holiday."

Yasmeena smiled and nodded. She knew that it was customary for many Kuwaitis to travel abroad for holidays every July or August, leaving their sweltering kingdom to seek cooler temperatures in pleasant vacation spots.

Lana further explained, "My father had previously scheduled important business meetings in London, so he felt compelled to keep those appointments. He took my two brothers with him. Mommy insisted that they leave and that we would follow as soon as my sister's sickness passed."

Lana loosed a ragged sigh. "Who could have known that Saddam's dispute with the Emir would erupt into war? Who could have known? Saddam is always quarrelling with somebody."

Yasmeena interjected, "I thought the same thing! One would think that he was weary of war after eight years of battling the Iranians."

"Anyhow, we never thought angry words would deteriorate into war. Our bags were packed and airline flights were rescheduled for August 4. But you know what happened. After the invasion, my mommy was trapped with her three daughters.

"After the Iraqis came, we should have joined other Kuwaitis who ran away." Lana smiled lightly. "There were lots of women whose husbands were out of the country. Those women didn't waste a moment. They loaded their cars and drove at full speed across the desert into Saudi Arabia. But Mommy hesitated. She attended the Haj pilgrimage to Mecca a few years ago and she remembered that Saudi women are banned from driving. She was afraid that we would be arrested when we crossed the border. She decided to stay in Kuwait and face the Iraqis instead."

Lana's sad expression grew sadder still. "And here I am."

Yasmeena made a little noise in her throat and patted Lana's arm. "We will survive this. We will, Lana."

Lana's dreamy state carried her thoughts back to the tumult of the invasion day and she pondered, "I wish I knew what happened to those brave Kuwaiti women. The last we saw of them their hair was twirling in the breeze, their loud voices were shouting at anything and anyone in their path, and their little children were screaming in excitement." She giggled. "They were women leaving on an adventure! It was quite a sight!"

Lana lapsed back into deep thought, gazed into nothing, momentarily forgetting her visitor. Lana finally spoke, "I often daydream my way out of this reality. I rework my past so that my future did not come to be. So many times I have thought of how different life would have been if only Mommy had found the courage to join the caravan of women in their trek across the desert. Perhaps it would have ended badly if we had lost our way. Perhaps we would have died of thirst. But possibly we would have made it through and would now be in London with Father, shopping for cute clothes at the famous Harrods department store and eating at good restaurants." Lana smiled widely, considering such an outcome.

Yasmeena thought that most importantly, Lana would have taken her virginity to her marriage bed and be spared the knowledge of what it was like to be raped daily by a creature whom she believed to be more beast than man.

Lana picked up her narrative, "My heart tells me that I will never know anything more of Kuwait. I will die with many unknowns filling my mind."

Lana eagerly shared her sad saga with her new friend Yasmeena, telling her that her father would never have allowed her to leave their home, no matter the emergency. But her panicked mother couldn't decide what to do. At their moment of crisis, she had spent a day or two frantically walking in circles and trying to phone Lana's father. A day later, her mother came down with her sister's same sickness; then they were truly stranded. When her mother grew more ill, she finally located a doctor who had cared for her children and he confirmed that she needed medicine. Only two weeks after the invasion, she reluctantly sent her oldest daughter with the family driver to pick up the medications ordered by her doctor and waiting at the local pharmacy. Normally the pharmacist would have dispatched his Palestinian delivery man to bring medicines to a favored client, but two days after the invasion that man had fled the country to return to his family home in Jordan.

"Mommy sent me on an errand to pick up her medicines. She had no idea what was happening outside our villa walls. We had walled ourselves inside, keeping our home dark and quiet, afraid to do anything more than peer from our windows. How could she know that Iraqi soldiers were plucking women from the streets?"

"Oh, Lana, I'm so sorry."

Lana brushed her off, still eager to confide in someone, anyone. "I was condemned from the moment I got out of our car to walk into the pharmacy. Suddenly a group of enemy soldiers stepped into my path. It was the first time I had seen them up close. They stared at me without speaking and then one of them grabbed me. Before I could scream, an immense hand was laid over my mouth and I was dragged away by three soldiers. Our driver probably never knew what happened. Mommy probably thinks I disappeared into the air."

A ragged sob broke from Lana, but she didn't shed tears.

Tears, however, were streaming down Yasmeena's face. Lana was so young, a mere child of sixteen years to Yasmeena's twenty-three. Yasmeena realized that her own situation could be much worse.

Suddenly the guard appeared, telling Yasmeena, "Come. Your time is gone."

Yasmeena knelt down to hug Lana, who was still in her same reclining position. "I am down the corridor, only a few steps. I will be back, Lana. I will. Be strong."

And with a heartfelt hug, Yasmeena disappeared from Lana like a vision lost.

Chapter Five: The Wolfman

It has been estimated that Iraqi soldiers raped at least 5,000 Kuwaiti women during Iraq's invasion of Kuwait.
—*Rape of women as an Instrument of War*
http://www.gistprobono.org/id189.html

After Yasmeena's departure, she continually fretted over Lana's situation, but with each visit she learned many details of her young friend's capture, imprisonment, and continued rapes.

To my readers: Lana confided the following to Yasmeena:
After being grabbed from the street and pushed into a military vehicle, rough hands pawed Lana's body as she was being driven through the streets of Kuwait City. She was pulled from the vehicle and into a prison, hustled into a cell numbered 11. A rough-faced soldier demanded her identification papers, but she had none. "My papers were left with our driver," she replied in a soft voice.

Without her papers, the soldiers knew nothing about her. Her name, age, home address and, most importantly, details about her family were unknown. But one soldier kept demanding to know her name and age. She was too frightened hold onto silence. Finally the truth burst out of her mouth in a rush. "My name is Lana. I am sixteen years old."

Her jailers were enthusiastic to learn her age. They knew that a sixteen year old Kuwaiti girl would be a virgin. She listened fearfully as the five soldiers discussed their good fortune at finding such a young girl. They had only run a small errand to purchase headache pills for one of the women they had kidnapped. One never knew what might be found on a casual outing when there were no controls to restrain their actions.

Finding herself in the clutches of pure evil, Lana was having difficulty taking a full breath. She watched the men, her small mouth opening and closing in disbelief, little knowing that she resembled a gasping fish pulled from the water. Even though in shock, she could not avoid comparing the men to each other. Four of the five men appeared normal. Three of the five could claim pleasant-looking features belonging to young men whom no one would guess could stoop so low as to rape innocent girls. Two were very young, no more than eighteen or nineteen. But one of the men was unlike any man Lana had ever seen. He was a large, intimidating man with scar-pocked skin. He stared at her with smirking hatred and made an obscene gesture, demonstrating something bad she was sure, although Lana was unsure of his meaning. She blushed and looked away.

Unbelievably, the men were discussing "who would have her." Since all five men had seen her at the same moment, they decided that there was nothing to do but to flip a coin, with the final winner taking the girl as his own. Two of the younger-looking men were the first to flip the coin. The winner flipped with the third man. The winner of that flip turned to the menacing man and they flipped the coin. Lana struggled for breath, her hands covering her mouth. She prayed to Allah that the foul man would not be the victor.

But he didn't lose.

Realizing he had won the exquisite beauty, the menacing man smiled for the first time, moving toward Lana with haste, as though he couldn't wait a moment longer before laying his hands on her.

The man was in the cell and coming at her before she had a chance to react. He was saying something but his words were practically unintelligible. He was shockingly aggressive, taking mere seconds to rip her clothes from her body. Since she had left babyhood behind, no man had ever seen Lana without her clothes. The man held her captive, his forearm pushed against her throat while with his other hand he removed his clothes.

Lana had never seen a naked man. She knew nothing about sex, although she understood that something secret occurred during the night hours between husbands and wives; but like most girls her age, she was too shy to ask questions and was content to wait until her mother thought it appropriate to tell her.

Lana could not believe that her life had turned with the flip of a coin, one moment with her protective mother and baby sisters, and the next standing in a prison cell with a stranger; a naked stranger at that. Lana had no idea what might be coming next but her breath was knocked from her body when the man pushed her down on the hard floor. She screamed, struggling as hard as a small girl could, but the man pushed her thighs apart and crawled in between her legs. After heaving and pushing for what seemed an eternity, he was in! Liquid gushed from her body and something told her that it was her blood. She couldn't stop screaming. She tried to claw his eyes with her fingernails, but he easily held both of her small hands in one of his own. She tried to kick but couldn't get in a position to do him harm. All she knew was that she *had* to get him out of her. Her insides felt crammed with the thing she had seen, the sensation of a length and thickness so huge that she thought it might burst from her stomach or shoot out of her throat, as scary aliens bursting from human bodies she had once seen in a horror film.

Before she blacked out she heard his voice quivering with excitement as he proclaimed, *"You belong to me!"*

At SURRA at the Shiakan Al-Farise Hall on March 24, 1991: Hopeful
Kuwaiti's gathered for the buses bringing some of the Kuwaiti
prisoners from Iraq back to their families.

Women waiting for loved ones. This young woman was waiting for her husband who had been taken off the streets of Kuwait on the last day of the occupation. Many Kuwaitis were snatched off the streets and taken as hostages with the fleeing Iraqi army.

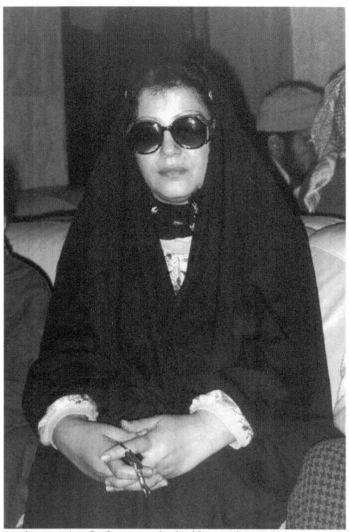

Mother waiting for her son who had been taken to Kuwait. He did not
return and is probably one of the 605 missing Kuwaitis who never
returned from Iraq.

(c) The Sasson Corporation

An emotional scene when a lost son is returned to his father after being starved and tortured in Iraqi prisons.
(c) The Sasson Corporation

Here are some real heroes, caretakers who gave no thought to their own safety but saved a home filled with disabled children.
(c) The Sasson Corporation
These photos are the property of The Sasson Corporation and are not to be duplicated or reprinted without permission.

Jean Sasson with happy boy who survived the occupation. There were many children in this home for disabled children but determined caretakers saved the children's lives after the Iraqi military took over the home and threw the children and the caretakers on the street.
(c) The Sasson Corporation

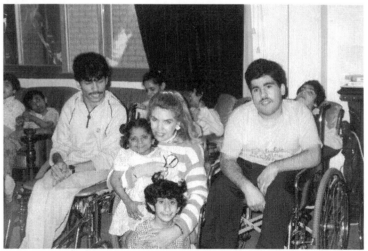

Jean Sasson with a group of children who survived the occupation.
(c) The Sasson Corporation

Southern Iraq where Jean Sasson and Soud a. Al-Mutawa sneaked into the country from Kuwait.

Jean Sasson and Soud Al-Mutawa explored Southern Iraq and chatted with the Iraqi people. Surprisingly, there was no tension between Kuwaiti Soud Al-Mutawa, and the Iraqis who greeted the author and Soud.

The author ponders, "What was this pensive Iraqi thinking as I took her photograph?" The author was in Southern Iraq after she slipped into the country from Kuwait.

Chapter Six: The Captain

Rape in war is not merely a matter of chance, of women victims being in the wrong place at the wrong time. Nor is it a question of sex. It is rather a question of power and control which is 'structured by male soldiers' notions of their masculine privilege, by the strength of the military's lines of command and by class and ethnic inequalities among women.
—*Rape and Sexual Abuse of Women in International Law*
http://www.law-lib.utoronto.ca/Diana/fulltext/chin2.htm

From that time, Yasmeena was allowed to visit Lana more than once. The Captain led her to believe that she could continue the visits. After meeting the hapless Lana, Yasmeena realized that her personal situation could easily be much more dismal that it was. In fact, in many ways she was luckier than the fourteen other young captives. In addition to being raped, most of the girls were routinely beaten. Anguished cries often reverberated like a storm roiling through the prison. Although the Captain was aggressive with her body, he didn't beat her. Although creepy, he had not yet become overly violent.

In fact, he had told her only the day before that he was going to have curtains hung from the ceiling to the floor, shielding her from the eyes of his men. She had smiled her first true smile since the day she was taken. When one is a prisoner, the smallest favors produce a surge of joy. She was eager for some privacy for solitude that did not exist. Anytime she crouched over the small pot that served as a toilet or washed her body with the water from the blue plastic pail, soldiers purposely walked past her cell so they might catch a good view of her breasts or shapely legs. For this reason, she often postponed using the toilet until pain made her fear her bladder might burst.

Despite her privileged position as the Captain's chosen sex slave, Yasmeena lived a life of terror. She spent many hours of the day and night nervously waiting for her rapist. Thankfully for Yasmeena, her rapist was also a military man, filled with self-importance in his role helping to subdue Kuwait and Kuwaitis. Therefore she was rarely raped more than once a day, which was a good thing. Most of the girls were raped more frequently, and none more often than poor Lana.

Waiting was particularly difficult because Yasmeena never knew what new deviant sexual idea the Captain might have gotten from his men or discovered while watching pornography films. He was using her lush body for fun, each day thinking of something new that he might do to her.

Yasmeena tried to stay mentally active, to keep her mind off reality, but what could a sex slave do in a barren cell but sit and relive the horror of being raped? After telling the Captain that she was going crazy sitting in a barren cell with nothing to do, he had presented her with a stack of fashion magazines and several paperback books. But serving as a sex slave meant that nothing of normal life could be properly grasped. Now she marveled that she had ever spent hours arranging her hair just so, and applying make-up as though perfection was something crucial for happiness, or complaining if her dress didn't hang just right on her figure. Now she knew that nothing she had previously believed essential was important at all.

Finally she gave up when she acknowledged that she could no longer comprehend what it was she was reading. Since then, the magazines had sat like useless stones in her cell.

The Captain and some of the other rapists had robbed some department stores and had gifted the girls with make-up, perfume, shampoo, soap and sexy nighties, saying they expected the girls to look good at all times. In his smug manner, the Captain told Yasmeena that he was a man who deserved the best, so he demanded that she look like a beauty queen or a movie star when he came in to rape her. She had to sit in the heat of the prison in full make-up, in case he popped in for a quick rape. He claimed to relish undressing her and delighted in her beautiful body each time he saw it.

Yasmeena was once again fretting over the horror of her new life when she heard the Captain's distinctive voice talking to one of his men. She caught deep breaths, trying to calm her nerves, bracing herself for sexual assault.

While Yasmeena was waiting to be raped, Lana began to screech, crying out, "Allah! Save me! Mother! Save me! Father! Save me!"

Several other female prisoners began shouting, "May God help you!"

The now familiar sounds of a physical beating, of fist pounding flesh, punctuated the loud screams.

The ricochet of so much human agony was unbearable to hear.

Just then, the Captain unlocked her cell door and walked in. Yasmeena could tell from the look on his face that he was angry about something. Perhaps it was the clamor emitted by anguished women. The Captain believed that all the women should peacefully, even gratefully, submit to their fate and make the best of it.

But these days his frustrations were generally evoked by setbacks in the military occupation. The task of making Kuwait the 19th province of Iraq was not going as smoothly as first planned. The Kuwaitis had renewed their rebellion, banding together for a riotous repulse and proving themselves unexpectedly clever and more powerful than a small group of untrained civilians should be. A second problem was the quick reaction by the United Kingdom's Prime Minister Margaret Thatcher and American President George Bush to call for Saddam's army to be routed. Since then, many countries sympathetic to the plight of the Kuwaitis had lined up with the Americans and the British, and were now gathering their armies in the nearby deserts of Saudi Arabia. All were promising to march across the desert and free Kuwait.

Despite the Captain's obvious foul mood, Yasmeena greeted him with her best fake smile. Her fear had eased recently. In spite of the Captain's total preoccupation in possessing and raping Yasmeena, up until this day, the captain had been the best among many bad men. But now he came at her a changed man. When she saw the fury on his face, it was clear he was going to take his anger out on her.

But she did exactly as she was ordered, undressing and bracing her elbows on the mat and raising her buttocks in the air. She had learned that the Captain liked raping her from all positions. But she was in for a terrible surprise, horrified when he began to rape her in a place forbidden.

She felt such immediate physical agony that she struggled to move away, but he clenched his fist and hit her on the head, silencing her screams. But the sexual act was so painful that she could not cease her soft groans and her cries blended with his excited moans and shouts to create a disagreeable symphony, a concerto of horror that would have never been written by Mozart or any other musical prodigy. Like a fog moving through her brain, she dimly discerned distant shouts and laughter, although the Captain's men didn't drift to the cell to gape at the sight of her naked brutalization, the way they did when other soldiers were raping their women. Yasmeena was saved from that degradation only because the Captain was the highest-ranking officer in this debauched circle of rapists.

After the Captain finally withdrew his body from her body, he hummed a casual tune as he cleaned himself with a bottle of water, splattering her with the excess then wiping himself with the edge of her blanket. He paused and asked in a soft sing-song tone, "Was that good for you?" When she didn't answer he grew annoyed, "I know you like it. I'm the best lover. I don't do the same things over and over. All the girls tell me that I am very imaginative."

She grunted a small sound that she hoped would be construed as a positive response by a man who imagined he was the greatest at everything, and who believed a woman being raped relished every minute of the attack. He used his foot to lightly brush against her bottom, a sign of affection from a man with no clue as to the reality of what he was doing. He didn't seem to notice when she cringed and pulled away.

He then sat and smoked a cigarette, waiting for her to wash her body because he loved taking in that scene. "After we have sex, I want you to serve me a cup of tea," he said, adding something new to their routine. He sat staring, never once taking his eyes from her body.

She did as she was told, pushing herself upright. Although every movement was agony, she fumbled to pick up her robe from the floor. He commanded her, "No. Do not cover yourself."

Humiliated and nude she found his tea cup and heated the hot water over the one-eyed burner, dropping in a tea bag from the cache the Captain had stolen from a Kuwaiti supermarket.

He never shifted his eyes from her body, but he was happy to sit sipping his tea, a man who loved a captive audience.

She attempted to slip on her robe once again but he said "No. Remain as you are."

71

"Please. Do you want your men to see me?"

"They are not so stupid. They will not look."

Yasmeena suddenly realized that when the Captain was in her cell, none of the soldiers came to their area. The Captain had obviously given orders that he was to have privacy.

And so she did as she was told.

And he began to talk, surprising her by talking about his wife who lived in their village in Iraqi. "My poor wife. She is still a young woman, but after seven children she has lost her beautiful body. She does not like sex and we keep out the lights when we do it, which is all right with me because her sagging breasts and belly is not something I want to see."

Yasmeena was suddenly and strangely struck with envy of the Captain's wife. It would be nice to have an unattractive body her Captain did not desire, and certainly it would be less embarrassing to be raped in darkness. She hated seeing his spooky eyes examining her body, scrutinizing every little crevice like he was studying for medical school exams.

But she heard little else because at the moment she could only think about the pain rippling from her rectum up through her stomach and chest. She had imagined that losing her virginity to this beast of a man was the most excruciating experience of her life, but it was nothing compared to this latest violation. She was in such physical agony that she shivered, feeling a chill on her flesh, a strange sensation in a desert dwelling without an air conditioner. The Iraqi soldiers had stolen Kuwaiti luxuries such as air conditioners during the first week of the occupation, and sent everything they could dismantle back into Iraq for the Iraqis. Now the building was so hot that Yasmeena often had difficulty taking a full breath. A fan blew directly into her cell but its blade had only hot air to move.

Just as she was thinking that he would never stop talking, he reached over and grabbed her breast, laughing when she jumped in pain.

Then he began to talk about his children. There were four girls and three boys. The girls would be married as soon as they were age thirteen. He could not risk any wicked conduct, behavior that would shame his good family name. He felt that his name was respected throughout his village and beyond. During his boring monologue he suddenly and roughly grabbed her by the neck and pulled her to him.

She gasped, pulling away.

He laughed again, telling her, "Admit it. You like little surprises."

His emotions scattered. Suddenly she heard him talk strangely, telling her, "You are a cold woman. I am a great lover and you never tell me. I know that you love me, but you never tell me." He shook his head in disappointment. "Do you not appreciate me?"

Yasmeena could not believe his words. Her rapist was preposterous in his thinking. Had he forgotten that she was kidnapped? Had he forgotten that she was a virgin who was being brutally raped by a man she did not know?

"You will please me or I will replace you." He paused and added menacingly, "You know what that means, Yasmeena."

Indeed she did. From what she observed on the first day of her imprisonment, she knew that women had been murdered at this prison.

"I know you love me. So, you must tell me. I know you find me attractive, so you must tell me. I know that you love the things we do, so you must tell me."

Although Yasmeena's tongue could barely move, she forced the lies from her trembling lips, whispering, "I love you." She paused, staring at his expectant expression, knowing that he would never be satisfied. "You are such a big, handsome man, any woman would love you." She was surprised that her tongue did not blacken and fall from her mouth at such a disgusting lie. Perhaps, she thought, she would never be able to speak again.

The Captain was pleased to hear her say what he thought he already knew. He smiled and talked until he could think of no more to say. Finally he stood up and said that he was leaving for a few hours, telling Yasmeena, "You are bleeding. I do not like to see all that blood. Clean yourself. I'll return later today and I want you to be ready for me. We are going to try something else new. I want you to wear the red gown." He paused, then reminded her yet again that she was disposable. "If you bore me, I will get another girl."

When she heard the metal door clang closed and his footsteps fade away, she went to a dark place in her mind. She decided that she must kill herself, despite the fact Muslims believe that suicide is an unforgivable sin.

Suicide was the answer. She was never going to get out of this hellish prison alive, anyway. In the three weeks she had lived there, she had heard of six girls that had been executed when their rapists replaced them with even younger girls. Her Captain had told her that at age twenty-three she was the oldest girl in the prison, and she wondered when the Captain would empty her cell for a new conquest, a virginal girl more beautiful. Certainly there were plenty of beautiful girls in Kuwait to kidnap, Yasmeena knew, for during her years of working as a stewardess she had seen them.

Yasmeena stifled her tears. She must be strong enough to end her life. Every girl and woman in the prison was going to die, anyhow. She might as well avoid weeks or months of torture and agony. She would commit suicide.

Chapter Seven: Suicide

Yasmeena quickly discovered that suicide is never easy. Particularly without a gun or a sharp instrument it isn't easy to terminate life.

Yet she knew that suicide was her best option. She was going to die, anyway. Most likely, the Captain was already wearying of her. Soon he would order her execution.

She thought about death for a very long time, reliving what she had just endured. She would rather die than be anally raped on a daily basis, and from the way her rapist had moaned and panted, she knew he had been more excited about this new carnality than any other defilement. This new kind of brutality bringing him so much pleasure was not something he would give up.

But her poor body could not withstand another anal rape. Everything back there felt raw. She really would rather be dead than to endure such anguish.

Blood still seeped from her rear, so she decided to clean herself up before dying and being buried. Even in death she would be embarrassed for gravediggers to see blood stains between her buttocks. Her fate of death by anal rape would be obvious. Those men would pause with shovels in hand to look at her face and commit it to memory. After the war when her parents came to Kuwait searching, waving photographs of their beloved daughter, they would be told that she had been raped to death in a place that should not be touched by any man. Then her parents, too, would die from the shame of their daughter's fate.

Yasmeena groaned as she lifted her washing pail and filled it with water. She placed the pail on the floor and lowered her bottom into the pail. The water triggered painful shocks to flare like a storm in her body. She pulled herself up and looked into the pail to see the water was bright red. Perhaps there was no need to kill herself. She was going to bleed to death.

After patting her bottom dry, she struggled to dress, moaning as she pulled the long t-shirt over her head. She attempted to slip on a pair of panties but she couldn't bear the pain of even soft fabric against her backside, so she discarded those and pulled her t-shirt down as far as it would cover.

Everything hurt. Suddenly she remembered her elderly grandmother. Yasmeena realized that her movements were as laborious as those of her grandmother when she attempted to dress without assistance from her daughter or granddaughters. Yasmeena decided that if she ever returned to her home in Lebanon, she would be more sympathetic to all her elderly relatives, including an auntie she had never really liked.

But now she had deathly serious matters on her mind. She studied the items in her cell, desperate to find an instrument lethal enough to end her life. There was pitifully little to choose from in her sparsely furnished jail cell. There was her sleeping mat and a dirty sheet and blanket and the few items associated with making tea. The tea was heated on an electric burner and she supposed that she could set her blanket aflame and wrap her body in that. Truthfully, though, she had feared fire since the day her mother told her about a despairing friend who had been married to an Arab from one of the Gulf nations, a man who came to Beirut to study. After only a short courtship he claimed to love her mother's friend, cleverly displaying a false mask professing adoration and promising her family that she would live like a princess in a luxurious villa staffed with servants. He was wealthy and he did have a big palace, but none of that luxury mattered after he turned into a brute within a few months of their marriage. He beat her if she asked to leave the villa to shop or to visit with some cousins. Later he brought home prostitutes and punched his wife in the face when she protested. With a broken nose and cracked teeth, she slipped out to call her mother and confided the problem: Her own mother told her to "be patient, my daughter," and to "make your husband happy so he will not need prostitutes."

With her mother's words ringing in her ears, the poor dear knew that she had nowhere else to turn, and so desperate to get away from her pitiless husband, in a rash moment she had doused herself with cooking kerosene and set herself on fire. The unfortunate darling didn't die as planned, but instead lived to suffer dreadfully. The attractive girl who once had long thick hair was left as bald as Yasmeena's aging grandfather, whose skull was skin slick and shiny. Her once sweet and pretty face was so scarred with lumps of shiny red flesh, that her toddler son failed to recognize her and screamed in fear when she made an appearance. Rebuffing her request for a divorce, her husband refused to send her home to her family.

Yasmeena's mother had heard he was enraged that his wife preferred death to life with him that he kept her near just so that he might taunt her. A second wife soon moved into the palace and the situation worsened when she claimed to lose her appetite at the sight of the pathetic creature. Finally the burned wife was ordered to live in one small room and was not allowed access to the rest of the house, even to be with her child. Without proper medical care, the poor dear died of an infection six months after her failed suicide.

No, that was not the end Yasmeena sought.

She noticed a bag of cookies and two apples that the Captain had given her and wondered if she might choke to death in swallowing a cookie whole. On second thought, that attempt might give her jailors time to rush in and beat on her back or yank the cookie out of her throat, so she discarded that idea, wanting them to keep their filthy hands away from her.

Her thoughts returned to the electric burner and her water bottle. She had once read in a magazine that women eager for male children killed female infants by pinching their mouths open with one hand and pouring scalding water down their throats with the other.

That might do the trick, she mused, though she quickly discarded that idea, too. She wished to die, but to die without a lot of suffering. From what she had just endured, she was not looking for more physical pain.

That's when she decided to suffocate herself with her mat. Smothering shouldn't be too excruciating. Yes, yes, she thought, as excited as she used to get on a sunny day at the beach in Jounieh, Beirut's picturesque seaside port area of magnificent Beirut. The Lebanese were the most fun-loving of all Arabs, gathering in sexy bikinis at the beach and capping the day with a delicious fish dinner at one of the many seaside restaurants. She laughed quietly for the first time in weeks. Yes, of course, she would asphyxiate herself.

Her backside was so painful that it took her many moments to stretch out next to her mat. Satisfied that none of the other rapists were spying on her cell, she gathered the thin bed mat over her head and held it tight against her mouth and face. For good measure she held her breath. Confident of her success, she enjoyed an image of her sweet mother's face, as well as the remainder of her family who appeared to say goodbye. Just as she thought the end was upon her, a life-saving breath came involuntarily. Still convinced that she could do this thing, she held the mat with one hand and groped with her other hand until she grasped the big tea pot, piling it on the top of the mat. But the heavy pot tumbled off and rolled about on the concrete floor. Thankfully, no one came to check on the clamor. Fifteen women being held prisoner and brutally raped generated a constant din, with many of the women screaming, while others wept loudly. A few of the braver women threw things around in their cell, and one woman had a habit of banging her brass coffee pot on the cell bars. Oddly, the woman's rapist didn't beat her for the habit, but instead ridiculed her for it and pledged to buy her a hearing aid after she clattered herself deaf.

In fact, all the rapists and jailers expressed amusement at the misery of the women, calling them crazy and teasing that the women needed raping continually. At those times, some of the men would go to the women, giving them what they so stupidly believed the women wanted, when in fact it was rape that was creating the anguished chaos in the first place. Yasmeena had difficulty grasping the thought processes of these rapists, men who truly seemed to believe that the women were grateful for being chosen as rape victims.

Still alive despite tucking a bunch of loose tea in her mouth and tightly wrapping her face with her skirt, Yasmeena burst into tears. She was going to live. It was impossible to kill herself without something lethal she could use as a weapon.

Sharp pain radiated from her backside and flared into agony when she tried to stand. She felt the area with her hand and realized that with the strain of trying to hold her breath, something important had burst and everything back there was wet with hot blood. Stymied with failure to end her life, Yasmeena curled on her mat, gathered her body into a fetal position, and wept.

Chapter Eight: Lana and the Beast

Suicide was not an option for Lana. At least that is what she told her friend Yasmeena. No, she had never considered suicide, although the thought of death was never far from her mind. Each time her rapist opened her cell door, Lana said, she presumed the monster was there to murder her.

Lana once whispered to Yasmeena that she believed God was interrupted during His creation of her rapist because he looked and acted like a genetic mutant. As Lana described his appearance, Yasmeena shuddered in disgust, learning that coarse black hair obscured his chest, stomach and back. He was a big man, more than a foot taller than Lana. His weight was triple her weight. His face was pitted with scars and his teeth were colored dark from years of smoking. Even his ears were eerie, standing straight out from the sides of his head like nothing Lana had ever seen. Had he been born in Kuwait, Lana believed, some charity would have provided the funds to tack those ears back to his head. And should any movie producer in America's Hollywood catch a glance of him, surely they would use him as the model for an evil cartoon character.

Lana confided that the rapist kept a raping schedule, coming to claim Lana's body each day at nine every morning, at three every afternoon and at midnight. His rape schedule never varied although his rape methods altered according to the time and to his mood. He seemed to take the most incredible joy from seeing her resist, watching her cry while she writhed in pain and pled with him to stop. Sometimes he would howl like a wolf at her cries of pain and terror.

◆ ◆ ◆

The Wolfman exuded a malevolent presence as insidious as a poisonous mist that penetrated the entire prison. Lana said that she could sense him before she saw him. When she felt his evil aura, she would sit upright, waiting to hear his thunderous footsteps. The Wolfman did nothing lightly. The Wolfman always arrived on schedule. Even if she was napping Lana would instantly wake up.

Lana once described this disturbing scene in great detail to Yasmeena:

Seconds after feeling his presence, the rapist slammed into her cell, his dark eyes sparking with hatred as he ordered, "Get naked."

Lana would obey no such order, she said. She slowly eased to her feet, still tender and sore from previous rapes; nevertheless, she would fight him, as she always did.

The beast glared as she stood staring, trying to control her racing heart. Face to face with the beast, her thoughts spun busily, trying to think of a new tactic to win one of their fights.

He slapped at her but missed when she jumped backward.

He clenched his fist and punched, connecting with her shoulder.

Her small body was thrown across the room, slumping against the block walls.

The beast laughed. "You can do nothing!"

He gripped her neck and pushed her head against the cinderblock wall. He kneed her in the stomach and when she doubled over, he tore at her clothing. The sound of ripping fabric was so exhilarating to him that his face distorted. Then something strange happened that Lana had never seen before. White foam bubbled from his mouth.

Lana froze in terror. Had her rapist been bitten by a rabid dog? Even before she was kidnapped, her mother had heard that pet dogs turned loose by the Iraqi invaders had gathered into packs and were roaming the streets. Perhaps wild animals had contaminated some of those dogs with rabies.

But she quickly shed that worry because she was naked, vulnerable to the beast's huge hands that roughly grabbed her body. He soon tired of the game and yanked off his pants before throwing her down to the mat to rape her.

Lana began to scream, her wails like those of her cat that had been torn to pieces in her brother's car engine the previous summer. Her anguished cries caused the beast to laugh with the high-pitched chatter of a buffoon. He shouted that her shrieks were the funniest thing he had ever heard.

Soon she had bigger worries.

The cells in this Kuwaiti neighborhood prison had been built in a single file, none facing the other. There could be visual privacy if a rapist desired seclusion while raping, although everyone in the prison could hear the screams of the individual women when they were being attacked. Although the rapists seemed to enjoy walking about and looking at the women, most of the rapists didn't allow their buddies to watch when they raped their prey. But now her rapist called out like an enthusiastic ringmaster, "Come and watch her take it!"

To Lana's despair, the men gathered, behaving like children at a circus. But this prison circus was nothing a child should ever attend. This circus was a place where cages were cells, and where women were turned into animals and forced to perform and entertain.

The excited soldiers whooped and shouted their approval of Lana's complete agony as she was flipped naked through the air and skewered like a piece of meat by the Wolfman's enormous male organ.

In many ways the Wolfman was like an actor who craved attention and ached for the approval of applauding spectators. An audience stirred his pride to swell along with his male appendage. Carried away by the cheering audience, he flipped her over and attacked her physically, biting her savagely from her face to her toes, like a starving tiger. The soldiers applauded when he ripped small pieces of flesh from her body with his teeth.

She crumpled into a blood-spattered heap, passing out although she quickly regained consciousness when he began to rape her yet again.

Finally he was finished. He waved the reluctant soldiers to leave. The circus was closing.

The beast slipped on his trousers and left the cell, returning with a cup of tea. While smoking a cigarette and drinking his tea, he began to rant about his hatred for everything Kuwait and Kuwaiti. He was resentful of the success of the little oil kingdom, while he lived under the failure of a huge oil kingdom. He was embittered by what he claimed was Kuwaiti smugness, and by the wealth that swept Kuwaitis to London and New York to spend more money in one day than he had seen in his lifetime.

"I hate every Kuwaiti," he sneered, mocking every Kuwaiti. "Why should Kuwaitis be rich and Iraqis be poor?"

His hatred was deep and real. Perhaps he actually did think he was punishing the Kuwaiti nation by kidnapping and raping young Kuwaiti girls. He could not slake his thirst for revenge even after raping her three times a day for 40 days. She had kept count by tearing small strips from papers in her cell and piling them in a corner, a strip for each day that passed. Just yesterday she had counted the strips. She knew now that she had been raped 120 times, each episode lasting at least an hour.

He looked at her and smirked, saying that that other rapists took care to moisten the private areas of their women with Vaseline to make sex easier. Nearly all the imprisoned women had been virgins when captured. He admitted that, "I like it when you scream. No Vaseline for you, Lana."

Although in pain, Lana sought of something she could say that would humanize her to her rapist, though she quickly realized no need to bother: The beast's words and actions betrayed a form of insanity. So she didn't mention that her family frequently took vacations in Basra, the beautiful Iraqi city of date trees, or that her parents held deep affection for a number of Iraqi families and educated people they had met when partying in South Iraq. She dared not tell him that she had often heard her parents discussing Iraq and Iraqis, her father acknowledging that the dictator's flaming oratory had at first captured the hearts of Iraqi citizens, although soon he simply frightened Iraqis into obedience. In her father's opinion, Iraqis for the most part were good people, albeit deeply unlucky with their brutal ruler, Saddam, and with the men of his tribe who supported him unconditionally. She had once overheard her father say that the rulers of Iraq were violent men who shot a man as easily as they plucked a date off a date tree, men who took everything for themselves, men who enjoyed the prolonged vivisection of the Iraqi people, a people whose energies were dissipated in the brutal daily task of survival.

Her rapist further terrified her when he began to think about her family. He asked, "Where do you live? Do you have sisters?"

"No. No sisters," Lana lied, her voice shaky.

"If you had sisters, I would go and get them."

Lana remembered that the beast started fantasizing, "Yes, I would put you and your sisters in a row. Then I'd give you all a good time." He could easily service the whole family of females, he claimed. Once, years ago, he had been selected to accompany his supervisor to Thailand to pick up some government items and while there he frequented a brothel in Bangkok, hiring the madam to bring him three young Thai virgins. One of them was only nine years old and the other two were thirteen or fourteen. He had given those virgins the best time of their lives. He mistook the horror on each child's face as pleasure. A wide grimace that he probably thought was an attractive smile covered his face.

A girl pure in morals but strong in feelings, Lana glowered at him, unable to restrain her revulsion one second longer. She shouted, "You are a beast!"

His anger burst over her like a tempest over the sea. He leapt on her once again, pushing her head on the floor, grabbing her small tongue in his huge hand. He pulled her tongue so hard she thought her tongue was going to be torn loose. He warned her, "If you insult me again, I will pull your tongue from your neck!"

Lana said nothing, chary of his anger.

He pulled away and stood to kick her in the stomach before reaching for rope he kept in a corner of the cell. He bound her for the first time, alarming Lana when he hung her by her arms and splayed from the ceiling fan. For fun, he flipped the fan switch. The fan spun slowly, making a low grinding noise. There she hung.

Looking like a madman with his eyes gleaming and his face furious, he snickered at her discomfort and terror, announcing that she would hang there while he went to prayer. It was time for the sunset prayer, so she knew he would be away a long time.

The beast left but soon other rapists gathered at her cell for a second time to gawk, making crude jokes and laughing loudly at the sight of her humiliating

85

position. She pleaded with them, "Please, cut me down. I beg you." The rapists ignored her pleas.

The beast Wolfman returned hours later, cutting the ropes and slamming her to the floor where he immediately began raping her.

As he raped, he ranted, cursing her and all Kuwaitis, "All Kuwaitis think they are kings. But that is over now," he told her, his voice as frightening as his man's part, his tongue wagging back and forth like a dancing snake, telling her hatefully, "Kuwait is no more. You Kuwaitis will now be our servants, the way you thought Iraqis were born to serve you!" His eyes ignited in sparkling pleasure with the thought that most delighted him, *"You will receive this every...day...of...your...miserable ...life."*

Lana closed her eyes from the utter terror, knowing that she was powerless to stop this man from using her body in any debauched manner he desired, and to use it anytime he wanted. She really was doomed.

Chapter Nine: Yasmeena's Choice

Confrontation in the Gulf: Iraq Seen Looting Kuwait of Identity:
"Having physically denuded Kuwait in nearly two months of military rule, looting computers, amusement-park rides and even street lamps and school blackboards, Iraq has embarked on a systematic effort to strip the nation of its very identity, exiled Kuwaitis and other recent refugees say. Since its invasion on August 2, they say, Iraq has seized or destroyed computer records of Kuwaiti citizens, cancelled and invalidated all Kuwaiti drivers' licenses, auto license plates and other means of identification...
The Kuwaitis who remain in their homes, many surviving on hidden stocks of food bought as the invasion began, have rallied in the face of occupation, according to Kuwaitis now in exile, organizing neighborhood groups to maintain public services and mounting a tiny but reportedly effective armed resistance."
—*The New York Times*
September 29, 1990

"My country is being savaged and destroyed, our women subjected to mass acts of rape, our men and even children are being murdered while these armchair analysts advocate waiting a year or up to 18 months for sanctions to force him out. Those who favor letting us suffer might at least consider calling upon Iraq to permit a human rights observer force to enter Kuwait – which they have refused to do – to protect our people there."

—Sheik Saud Nasir al-Sabah, Kuwaiti Ambassador to the United States
October 1990

After failing to commit suicide, a nervous Yasmeena sat waiting in her red lacy nightie, wondering what kind of new sexual assault she must endure. She had given up thoughts of suicide and since she was not dead, she wanted to live. She decided that the time had come for her to make a choice between living or dying. Yasmeena's choice was to live.

While considering her options, she recalled the many times her father had told her that she was an unusually intelligent girl. She must use that intelligence to outwit the captain. The Captain was a man so in love with himself that he could be manipulated. She would manipulate him into loving her.

But first she must stop the life-threatening anal assaults, or she would wither and die, unable to find the energy to outmaneuver the captain. So first she would appeal to the Captain, reminding him that she was a physically small woman in every way and that his large male part had hurt her terribly. She would praise him for his abilities as a great lover, showering him with compliments because he liked nothing more than hearing how exceptional he was. Perhaps his heart would soften and he would take pity on her.

Truthfully, she didn't know anything about true love and sexual relationships between a man and a woman. She only knew about being raped. The Captain was the first man she had ever seen naked, other than the time a cousin had been visiting at their villa in Beirut. The poor lad was in the toilet when Israeli planes had flown over the city on a mission to sow panic in Lebanese citizens. When one of the planes triggered a sonic boom, her spooked cousin had shot out of the toilet with his penis in his hand. She had felt a rush of embarrassment layered with curiosity, but she didn't see much because he was an undeveloped youngster and his hand had pretty much covered everything.

When the Captain failed to return, Yasmeena was treated to a rare moment of happiness when a soldier told her the Captain would not return to the prison until the following morning. He had been called to headquarters, wherever that might be.

This news tweaked everyone with curiosity. Yasmeena listened carefully as the soldiers discussed the latest rumors from Baghdad. The Kuwaiti fighters had recently blown up several buildings housing enemy soldiers. They had also ambushed and killed an Iraqi team of five men. Saddam was furious. The soldiers gossiped for an hour or so, their loud voices ringing through the prison, speculating that Saddam had sent orders for them to clamp down harder on the Kuwaitis.

Yasmeena pondered what more the Iraqis could do to the Kuwaitis. They had already taken over their country, burglarized their businesses and homes, murdered many young men, and raped and murdered women.

Finally the bored men wandered into the various cells, raping their women, whose muted cries rang throughout the prison.

Inside the Kuwaiti Resistance

Assignment: During the Gulf War, there were fragmented reports of a sophisticated resistance movement operating in Kuwait. Newsweek wanted to know more. After canvassing Americans who had escaped Kuwait, I found one who (reliably) claimed to have been involved and could provide details.

While declining to provide specific numbers, Rickert claims the resistance "is run by a few military men and a lot of businessmen, with some individuals who've just volunteered. I'd say 98 percent of it is Kuwaiti....It's lots and lots of people everywhere, more people than you would believe....They're resisting every way they can." Many in the Kuwaiti military, Rickert notes, were executed during the first days of the invasion. Those who escaped did so with forged identification.
—*Newsweek*
Dec. 20, 1990

After the evening's rapes were finished and the women's sobs diminished, Yasmeena anticipated a restful sleep. For the first night since her capture, she was sure she would not be awakened by the Captain and forced to endure a painful assault. No matter how many times he raped her, each time felt like the first time, as shame and humiliation tore at her alongside the agony.

She slipped off the red nightie that suddenly felt repulsive on her body to pull on a light-weight t-shirt and slacks, feeling better than she had felt in hours. She slipped under her new pink blanket, a present from the Captain. She took a long, relaxed breath.

She lay quietly, thinking about the brave Kuwaiti fighters, wishing that she was free to assist them once again. After discovering first-hand the cruelty of the occupiers, she prayed that the Kuwaitis were enjoying success after success. Surely they must be conducting deadly attacks to have spurred a studied reaction from Baghdad. She was curious to know more details, but went to sleep knowing that she would find out soon enough: As the days passed, the Captain had grown entranced by his own voice and delighted in his one-woman audience.

Yasmeena had no doubt that the Captain would tell all when he returned from headquarters.

According to what he revealed, she might pass the information to Lana, in the hope that it would lift her spirits. The poor girl was at the end of her spiritual and physical strength, believing that she would never be liberated, and that the fleshly assaults would end only when her rapist murdered her.

And so Yasmeena slept more deeply than usual, when she was awakened in a few hours by screams; heartrending shrieks that could come only from one person. Lana! Poor Lana was enduring the usual midnight rape.

Yasmeena covered her ears with her hands and buried her head beneath the mat, but nothing could shut out Lana's wails. Yasmeena peered from under the blanket at the clock on the table, timing the assault as the long minutes ticked by: An hour and twenty minutes. Lana's violator had managed to rape his victim even longer than usual. Yasmeena knew that many of the other girls in the prison felt sorrier for Lana than they did for themselves. They made this clear by shouting out their regret and sorrow for Lana's situation, telling the young girl to, "Be strong," and "Allah will save you!"

There were times that Yasmeena thought Lana's screams were the only thing that kept the other rape victims alive. When compared to Lana's torture, all remembered their good fortune not to be the female chosen by Lana's rapist.

Yasmeena finally heard the unmistakable footsteps of Lana's rapist. He was leaving the prison. Yasmeena feigned sleep but narrowed open her eyes to watch Lana's rapist walk past, his gait so casual he might have been an ordinary man enjoying a waterfront stroll rather than a demon who took pleasure in repeatedly torturing a sixteen-year-old girl.

She recoiled as the beast paused to adjust his penis in his pants. That single glimpse reminded Yasmeena of the ghastly details the Captain once told her about the beast.

Lana's rapist was the most sadistic of all the men, and according to her Captain, a man with a terrifying weapon tucked in his pants, a penis so large that the other rapists jokingly called him "Akbar Zib" or "biggest dick."

Yasmeena would never forget the look of awe on her Captain's face when he described the beast's penis. The Captain claimed it was even bigger than his Uncle Nassar's penis, which was so gigantic that Nassar's poor wife ran shrieking from room to room trying to run away anytime Nassar demanded his marital rights. Once she had tried to escape from a window, but Nassar had caught her with her head dangling out and her backside in the house and he had given it to her right there.

Women living in nearby homes had peeked from their windows to locate the source of the racket. All that was visible to them was Nassar's wife, dangling from a window, her face contorting along with her shrieks. One of the women later gossiped that the sight was the funniest thing she had ever seen. She was only sorry that she did not own a video camera like they used in Bollywood. The scene could have been a comedic movie for all to enjoy, more entertaining in fact than the movie she had watched at the movie house in Baghdad when she had traveled there to visit her cousin.

Since the women did not know about Nassar's gigantic private weapon, they assumed that their neighbor was being beaten for spending too much money, or for overcooking the night meal; the usual, boring transgressions that earned a woman a beating in Iraq.

Just thinking of how the monster rapist pained the tiny Lana, she buried her head in her arms, wanting to weep for her friend, but by this time, Yasmeena was a woman who had run out of tears.

Lana was in her thoughts for hours. She had grown to love the Kuwaiti girl, considering Lana a younger sister, a sister she must protect. But protecting someone as beautiful as Lana, in a prison full of rapists, would be difficult if not impossible. Yasmeena could understand how Lana's beauty had inflamed all the rapists, causing grown men to flip coins in the hope of "possessing" her. Yasmeena knew that if the monster rapist tired of her, the other rapists would likely make an exception in Lana's case: She would *not* be shot. Those soldiers would start tossing coins once again and she would be passed to yet another soldier to do with her as he pleased.

But Lana's beauty was not her main appeal, at least not to Yasmeena. She was a young girl who had managed to keep her innocence while in the midst of evil most foul. Even when in severe pain, Lana greeted Yasmeena with the most gentle, sweet smile, solicitous always for Yasmeena's well-being.

Lana's cries slowly quieted, but Yasmeena could not drive from her thoughts the image of what Lana had endured. Finding sleep impossible, she finally moved from her mat to prepare a cup of hot tea.

While sipping the tea, Yasmeena considered once more her new situation. She believed that the Captain was entering a new and dangerous phase. He had been raping her for weeks and increasingly he appeared bored. His boredom spawned dangerous aggression that ultimately had culminated in anal rape. Yasmeena knew that she could not endure anal sex on a daily basis.

One man alone held her life in his hands and that man was her Captain. If his boredom continued, Yasmeena knew that she would be shot, just like the two Kuwaiti girls before her. The man in control of her body must want her to live; otherwise, she would die. To the Captain she was not a young woman with dreams and plans, but was merely a female body with desirable parts that he might abuse at will. She just happened to have a head atop her body, a head which was of no interest to the Captain.

Yasmeena's choice to live meant that she must hone her acting skills. She must become a talented actress in order to inspire her Captain to fall in love. Unless he grew to love her, another girl would soon occupy her cell while her body rotted in her grave.

That's when Yasmeena remembered The *Thousand and One Nights*, the story of Queen Scheherazade and her husband, King Shahryar. Yasmeena's mother had told her the story when she was a young girl, about a clever Queen who tricked her king.

The story was that when King Shahryar discovered that his wife had been unfaithful, he had her executed. In his grief and anger, he began to marry a succession of virgins. He was so convinced that all women were unfaithful that every virgin was executed the morning after her wedding night. When he could find no virgins left to marry, he turned to his vizier, Scheherazade's father, and demanded the vizier's daughter.

But Scheherazade was a cunning girl and on her wedding night, she told her king a fairytale, but refused to tell him the ending. Each night she would do the same thing. She would start the tale, but not finish it. Her king kept postponing her execution so that he could hear the conclusion. This went on for 1,001 nights.

Yasmeena thought about Scheherazade for a long time. The young woman had discovered the weakness in her king, that he loved hearing stories and once into a story, must know the ending. Yasmeena knew by this time that her Captain cared only for raping and sex. So she would become a vamp, a woman who would entice the Captain with her body, a tactic she hoped would keep him sufficiently intrigued to keep her alive.

Yasmeena would stop whining and begging, and instead become an expert on her Captain and on the prison that was now her home. She would observe everything around her, picking up on the rhythm of the sex prison, eavesdropping on the soldiers at every opportunity.

The following day, when the Captain came into her cell he was in a jovial mood. No doubt he was thinking of raping Yasmeena in the same manner as he had done during the previous visit.

The urgency of this immediate danger accelerated Yasmeena's strategy. The choice to live had now been rehearsed in her mind so many times before, now appearing to her as a carefully organized blueprint.

"My Captain," she said, "I would like permission to talk to you about something very important."

She waited for a physical sign that she could continue.

He stared at her, his brow furrowed. Finally he nodded, indicating his permission.

"Over the past few weeks I have come to see you a special man. I do want to please you. I do care about you. But my Captain, a wounded woman cannot be sexy. How can I be desirable if I am in pain?"

The Captain sat impassively, now smoking a cigarette.

Yasmeena's voice sounded very calm, although her heart was racing. "My Captain, your body is very large. Mine is very small. Your male organ is very large. My private parts are very small. It is very difficult to cram such a large item into such a small opening without causing a lot of damage."

She pretended to have feelings she did not, stroking his arm and telling him, "I have learned to appreciate sex and how good it is. But is best when we have sex in the normal manner, the way God intended men and women to come together."

The Captain suddenly looked pleased when Yasmeena lightly touched his genital area and whispered that, "You are the best man in all of Kuwait. I am lucky that you chose me." She hesitated, gathering her strength before adding her biggest lie, "I think my feelings are growing strong for you." She blushed and looked down, "Have you ever thought of taking a second wife?"

The captain did not look particularly surprised, for he was convinced he had the skills of an unrivalled lover, a Casanova, although he did toss back his head and laughed loudly, savoring the moment. He then looked at Yasmeena and declared, "I have been thinking of taking a second wife." He winked, "Now I have the money."

Yasmeena forced a smile, pretending that the Captain was her dream man. While her face wore an expression of obedient submission, her fertile mind was active, sated with loathing for him and every Iraqi soldier in Kuwait. Of course, he had the money, she thought to herself, as most of the Iraqi soldiers had been robbing Kuwait and Kuwaitis for weeks now. Many Kuwaitis living in Kuwait City were exceptionally prosperous, their homes filled with costly items and with huge safes crammed with expensive jewels, at least that was the case before the Iraqi locusts settled on the city, stripping Kuwait City bare.

The Captain promised, "I will take care for you, my sweetie. I will not hurt you if possible, Inshallah."

After their conversation, and after Yasmeena put into action her new role as a desirable woman who could not get enough sex, Yasmeena's life improved immensely. The captain was as happy as a groom establishing a home for his bride. That day he ordered curtains hung across the bars of her cell, and threatened his slack-jawed men that if they dared to look at his woman, they would regret it. A small wooden cabinet was brought in, and a variety of tasty food items Yasmeena had not seen for weeks were stacked on those shelves. A supply of music tapes featuring the most popular Arab singers was delivered. Other items were soon moved into her cell, including an easy chair, a floor fan to supplement the ceiling fan, a small refrigerator, a hotplate for cooking, as well as two tables and two straight-backed chairs. A large basin replaced the plastic bucket for her bathing convenience, and a plastic curtain was draped around her toilet area. Yasmeena's cell was suddenly overflowing with handy items meant to ease her imprisonment.

Yasmeena noticed that the Captain's rambling walk had ripened into a peacock strut. He was proud that his rape victim had fallen in love with him and was agreeable to marriage. As the days slowly ticked past, Yasmeena's worries about death slowly evaporated. She could see that her ploy was working on the Captain like a magician's wand. When he began stealing designer clothes for the two of them, she knew that he had made plans to take her home to Iraq to parade in his village. No man in that tiny Iraqi village would have a beauty like her as his second wife.

Despite her relief at knowing he would not now order her execution, and optimistic he would never again rape her in her anal area, she found that pretending to love the man who raped her was the most difficult thing she had ever done. The deception was almost as painful as the rapes. Inwardly she recoiled at his touch, but outwardly she displayed pleasure and joy each time she was raped. She even instigated sex, often surprising him after being raped by pleading with him to "do it again." Yet Yasmeena knew that she was playing a dangerous game, and if the Captain ever suspected her true motive for her declaration of love, he would shoot her himself, rather than depend upon one of his soldiers.

As the days passed, Yasmeena grew an expert at spying, at pretending to read or clean her cell while she listened to the soldiers gossip about their lives as rapists. Yasmeena learned that there was a clear plan to the structure of their sex prison, a structure laid out by the Captain. From the beginning, all of the men were allowed to choose one specific woman, and that woman was his, to do with as he pleased. The rapists never shared their victims. Each rapist was not allowed to tell another rapist how to treat his woman. All were free to rape, to torture, to murder, and no one would question them.

Only one thing was forbidden to them and that was the freedom to talk to outsiders about their women. They could not divulge details of their sexual slaves to anyone out of their close-knit circle, not even to other Iraqi soldiers. The Captain kept Iraqi soldiers from other units away; he shrugged and advised curiosity-seekers that his was a special facility for dangerous prisoners, and that he had specific orders to keep all from entering.

By keeping their sordid behaviors a secret, they seemed to believe that their acts were not crimes.

By this time there were so many Kuwaitis being held prisoner all over the city that no soldier questioned another. The Iraqi army was like a massive monster set down directly top of Kuwait City, a monster with long arms that stretched into every neighborhood. The Iraqi soldiers were free to rob, rape, torture and murder and no one would hold them accountable.

Yasmeena learned that there were other, more chilling, rules in the sex prison. When a rapist desired a new girl to rape, he must honor the Captain's orders that there would be no witnesses to describe the fate befalling female victims. So anytime a girl was "used up," she would be executed. No woman would be set free to detail the existence regarding the rape prisons. The Captain held a growing respect for the tenacity of the Kuwaitis. If Kuwaiti men learned what was happening to innocent women, that knowledge might initiate an attack upon the prison.

So the women were to be raped, and once their desirability faded, they would be murdered. The Captain was a clever man and acknowledged that it might be problematic for a man to execute the woman he had raped for weeks, so it was determined that the rapist's friends would shoot and kill any girl no longer desired. A stranger to the used-up girl would then drag her out, shove her to the small enclosed corner behind the prison, tie her to the executor's pole, and shoot her.

Once when in an angry mood after Yasmeena had underperformed during their sexual session, the Captain warned her, "There is a tall pole behind the prison, the kind you see in the old military movies where spies were shot. We tie the girls to that pole before execution."

Yasmeena never heard where the girls were buried. Once she overheard one of the soldiers brag he took the bodies of two dead girls and deposited them in garbage cans in front of a storefront. With the terrifying cloud of execution hanging over her head, Yasmeena was too nervous to ask the Captain where the girls were buried. She really did not want to know.

(The Rigga Cemetery is 18 miles south of Kuwait City. Iraqi soldiers were known to dump victims, including rape victims, near garbage cans or dump them at local cemeteries. The following is an article about this habit, written after Kuwait was liberated.)

Rows of fresh graves in Kuwaiti cemetery bear silent witness to Iraqi atrocities:

"Every fresh mound in Rigga cemetery tells a story. Mr. Mohammed tells those stories in calm, reasonable tones as he walks among the graves."
—*The Baltimore Sun*
March 4, 1991

Yasmeena knew she could not expect help from anyone. She was helping herself. Now, she wished only she might help Lana and the other women, too.

The young girls or women that had been captured were, for the most part, beautiful, since unattractive women were not kidnapped to be raped. Some of the women were educated and beautiful, women who would have married prominent men in their respective societies, whether Kuwaiti or Lebanese or Saudi.

The rapists were excited, finding themselves with beautiful women who would never give them a second glance in a normal setting. Like children in a candy store, the rapists were delighted by their good luck, thrilled with the knowledge that they could take any woman they wanted, and were free to enjoy any sexual pleasure.

With ruthless men freely raping terrified women, nothing of normal life could be found inside the walls of the prison circus.

Chapter Ten: Walking on a Tight Wire

Kuwait Refugees tell of Iraqi Killings and Rape

New refugees arriving here after fleeing Kuwait have offered emotional accounts of continuing Iraqi killings, rapes, torture and forced evacuation of civilians. The victims include a 12-year-old girl who was sexually attacked two weeks ago, according to a detailed account provided by a Kuwaiti doctor who said she had tended the abused child.... "The incidence of rape is now increasing in a pattern that seems to be repeated, like a contagious disease," she said. "Iraqi soldiers enter a home, tie up the men, rob the valuables and then rape the women. Most of the women I saw were molested and then sodomized," the doctor said. "When I saw them, they were in a state of shock, still denying what had happened to them." The doctor said the 12-year-old girl had been attacked by an Iraqi soldier who was one of a group that entered her home in the suburb of Bayan in Kuwait City two weeks ago.

—*The New York Times*
December 2, 1990

There are times of horror when specific events merge with human emotions and cause a person to temporarily become insane.

This happened to Yasmeena one afternoon while painting her nails with the nail polish given to her by the Captain. The vivid color was the Captain's favorite, ruby red. Her tipping point from sanity to insanity crept upon her, instigated by Lana's piercing screams.

Those screams pierced the air with an intensity that was shattering to anyone with a feeling heart. Yasmeena shook her head and drew a deep breath, thinking to herself that Lana's screams were so high-pitched and deafening that if their guards held a contest, the combined cries of the other fourteen imprisoned women could not compete with those of this one small woman. Poor Lana would win a crown no female would ever want.

Yasmeena glanced at the garish clock the captain had stolen from a jewelry shop to place on a table outside her cell. It was 3 o'clock in the afternoon, time for Lana's second rape of the day.

Even before Yasmeena saw Lana, she had suffered along with the unknown girl. Now, knowing something of Lana and of the beast, Lana's unsettling cries inspired the most unbearable images in Yasmeena's mind. Everything about Lana was so petite and delicate, while the beast was giant-sized and ferocious.

As Lana's wild shrieks intensified, insanity slithered from Lana's cell to Yasmeena's own. Her hands began to tremble, though that alone was not unusual. But when shivers snaked from her wrists up the length of her arms and into her shoulders and wormed into her neck, Yasmeena knew that she was in trouble. The spasms locked into her neck and her entire body started shaking uncontrollably, reminding her of the time she had once gone into a funhouse at a fair in Beirut. How she had laughed as she swayed from side to side, but on this occasion, body rocking was not a laughable matter.

When Lana's screams tipped to a new intensity, Yasmeena felt her own sanity slipping away. "Stop," she moaned. "Stop, stop, stop, oh please stop."

She must do *something* to stop Lana's screams and halt her own slide into madness, but she could do nothing because she was locked in a cell, unable to help her friend padlocked in another cell and being raped to death by the most gigantic penis known to men who took great stock by such things.

"Someone stop him," she pleaded, before flinging her nail polish to the floor and jumping to her feet. Without knowing how it happened, she felt her body moving, leaping up and down like a donkey trotting on sizzling embers.

Things got worse by the moment. Yasmeena had been physically swift and agile since childhood but suddenly her entire body was frenziedly contorting. If one didn't know better, one would believe that Yasmeena was being threatened by Lana's beast.

One of the rapists happened to walk past. Although the Captain had forbidden all his men from looking at Yasmeena, her extraordinary antics made it impossible for him to do otherwise. He stopped, he stood, and he stared. Amused, he called to his comrades. The rapists rushed to outside her cell, gathering in a circle to snicker at her extraordinary movements.

One of the rapist called out, "What is this? Is she a circus performer?"

Yasmeena did put on an entertaining show. One moment she was clutching the bars in her cell. The next moment she was trying to climb the wall, cramming her pointed toes into the cracks in the concrete. She lost all touch with reality and poked her head under her mattress, her rear thrust in the air. That unnatural pose brought howls of laughter from brutes who were jailors.

A second rapist agreed, "She must be one of those freaks who can twist their bodies like pretzels. I saw one of those acts when a circus from Budapest played in Baghdad."

"We have our own circus," a short and overweight rapist snorted. "Perhaps we can take this performer back to Baghdad and sell tickets."

When Yasmeena coiled her body into the shape of an S, evil guffaws snapped her back from her moment of madness. She collapsed on her mat and pulled her thin blanket over her shaking body and flushed face. Dizzy from her exertions, she whispered lowly, wondering, "What happened?"

Hearing the rapists excitedly debate her strange behavior and weird contortions, she realized that she had mentally gone somewhere unknown even to herself. She questioned if perhaps she had behaved like some of the wretched inmates at "The Birdcage," the notorious institution in Beirut built especially for the insane. Her medical doctor cousin had told Yasmeena about that strange establishment and she had listened attentively to his graphic descriptions of the patients' bizarre activities and their extraordinary physical capabilities.

Yasmeena feared that if she was not soon rescued from the prison circus, upon her return to Lebanon she would qualify for a bed in that very asylum. Perhaps her cousin would be the admitting physician. Then she could sit in a corner all day and relive the terrors of this sex-slave life, for most of the inmates there lived in their haunted pasts.

Her thoughts returned to the present when the rapists reluctantly dispersed to go about their business.

By this time, Lana's screams had subsided to a low moan.

Yasmeena turned over to her side, once again plotting how she could help herself, and all the other girls. Although such an achievement would take a miracle, Yasmeena believed in miracles.

Yasmeena's choice to do what she must do to survive sharpened once the Captain displayed signs of new-found love. Her false affection was swaying his feelings and behavior. According to the Captain, even his wife at home in Iraq had never seemed particularly thrilled when he insisted on sex. But clearly he regretted telling Yasmeena that little secret the instant he spoke the words. "Of course," he added, "she is the mother of my seven children and she keeps my home clean and food on my table. It is right that she deserves rest at the end of the day."

A few days later, after a particularly long session of raping Yasmeena, the Captain shared his plan of commandeering a villa in Kuwait City where they might set up housekeeping, although he had to be careful. His Colonel might hear of the set-up. Although his Colonel had no qualms about the soldiers kidnapping and raping women in Kuwait, he would not approve any of his men falling in love with the women, and certainly would not authorize marriage. The Colonel was so frightened of Saddam that he wanted nothing to happen that might cause friction with Baghdad. While Saddam detested the Kuwaitis and any other people living in Kuwait, and would never punish any soldier who committed violence against the enemy, he would not look fondly on his soldiers bringing home captive women as wives.

So the Captain had to take his time and devise a careful plan before he could bestow upon Yasmeena the honor of becoming his second wife.

And so her efforts won her a victory. Yasmeena was now seen by the Captain as a human being, and not as a mere receptacle for his male thing. She received small favors. She most wanted the freedom to visit Lana frequently, anytime the two women were not being raped. She was pleased when the Captain readily agreed with her request. He quickly directed his men to escort Yasmeena to Lana's cell once a day at five o'clock in the afternoon, two hours after Lana's three o'clock rape and seven hours before her midnight rape.

When Yasmeena casually mentioned that she was feeling tender and sore from his big male part, he sent four of his men into the city to steal various topical creams and pain medicines. The men, wanting to please their Captain, came back with a big supply of medications. When Yasmeena asked if she might distribute some of the medicines to the other women, he surprisingly agreed.

The following day Yasmeena took stock of her supplies. She packed several of each item into a small bag the Captain had given her to store her make-up. She also slipped in packages of cookies and other treats. She had often heard some of the girls calling out for food. Their younger rapists were so excited over unlimited sex they often forgot to supply food to the women.

Yasmeena pulled her shoulder-length hair into a pony tail, slipped in a modest dress and selected a new pair of summer sandals stolen for her by the Captain, before calling out to the guards. "Please, let me out. I am to be allowed freedom to go to the women."

Clean from a bath, and dressed nicely, and now going to visit the other women, Yasmeena felt almost normal for the first time since being kidnapped, although she also felt a web of guilt binding her thoughts. She was the only woman receiving such favors.

Two of the rapists came quickly, unlocking the cell door and standing back respectfully for Yasmeena to walk from her prison cell. Despite her antics that had so amused the rapists, the soldiers never dared mention that day to the Captain or to Yasmeena. Now they appeared eager for a chance to be of service, for their Captain had warned them not to display any aggression toward his woman.

106

Actually, they seemed inquisitive about Yasmeena. They were subordinates wondering that their Captain had lost his head over the girl. Yasmeena was very pretty, and had the biggest and most beautiful breasts in the prison, but her beauty did not match that of Lana's or even that of several of the other younger women.

Yasmeena knew why the men were curious. The Captain's men, and the other women, had noticed that for the first time, a woman was being treated like a favored guest at the prison, rather than a prisoner.

Only Yasmeena knew the shameful secret for her privilege. She was pretending to love the man who was raping her. But she had more important matters on her mind so she pushed her dishonorable conduct out of her mind. At the moment, she was infused with the seemly courage of a woman who was going to help other women.

Delivering the pain-relief medications to the suffering women, Yasmeena felt herself a modern-day Florence Nightingale, the celebrated English nurse who had first become famous during the Crimean War. Yasmeena had been taught about the devoted nurse during her school years in Beirut and remembered that she had been born into a wealthy English family living in Florence, Italy. She was named after the beautiful city and was expected to live the leisurely life of a society woman. But she had scorned that life and dedicated herself to helping others.

Yasmeena had a quick thought that she too would devote herself to some good cause, if she could only survive the madness of the prison circus.

Other than Lana, Yasmeena had never spoken with the other women. Even now, she would not be allowed to visit with them in their cells, though she was allowed to distribute medicines and foods to them.

Every woman was startled by Yasmeena's arrival. All were obviously in pain and distress and eagerly grabbed the medication and the food treats offered. That's when Yasmeena discovered that nine of the girls were Kuwaiti, and three were Filipina. Every woman was young. The Kuwaitis were schoolgirls, too bold for their own good as most had been kidnapped while out driving with their friends, thinking to check out the city under the occupation. The Filipina prisoners were housemaids to the Kuwaitis, poor women who had been taken by the soldiers while running errands for their employees. None of the women looked well, which was no surprise to Yasmeena.

Yasmeena's heart fluttered nervously when she passed two empty cubicles near Lana's cell. Earlier in the day, she had heard the sounds of two young women pleading for their lives, their pitiful appeals quickly followed by the sound of gunfire. She knew nothing much about those prisoners, other than they were Arab women who had met a bitter end.

Besides Yasmeena, there were now only twelve other women in the cells, down from fifteen prisoners. The incident reinforced her determination to manipulate the Captain with false words and gestures of affection. As difficult as it was to demonstrate false pleasure at being raped, it was the only way to come out of the prison alive.

Yasmeena stumbled in shock when she came to Lana's cell. The sight before her was too gruesome to believe, yet it was Lana's reality. The young Kuwaiti girl was naked on her mat. It was impossible for her to cover her body because she was trussed into immobility. Her hands were bound together over her head. Her legs were spread open and blood was pooled between her legs. Each ankle was tied separately to a cell bar.

Yasmeena gasped. Lana's face was swollen and dried blood was caked on her lips.

Lana's pleading eyes met Yasmeena's own, but she made no sound, simply blinking her eyes once in recognition.

Yasmeena thought that Lana might be dying.

108

The guards exchanged looks of shame at Lana's condition, although they were brutes nearly as depraved as Lana's rapist. At least they had the decency to look embarrassed, muttering to themselves as they unlocked the door and signaling with their hands for Yasmeena to enter. The oldest one warned Yasmeena, "Do not untie her." The youngest of the two rapists confirmed the reality of the rules that bound them all, "She is not our business."

Yasmeena growled softly under her breath. Every rapist was a king in the prison circus.

Yasmeena rushed into the cell, placing her medical supplies on the floor, and kneeling beside the young Kuwaiti, cradling Lana's head in her hands. Clearly, Lana had taken a terrible beating. Now that she was close, Yasmeena could see the full damage. The Kuwait girl's face was bruised, with one eye swollen and bruised. Her nose appeared to be broken, with dried blood crusted inside her nostrils. The girl's lips were swollen and so dry that they were split open in several places. Yasmeena's eyes quickly scanned Lana's body. Her neck was also badly bruised and Yasmeena could see that the bruises were in the shape of fingers, as though her rapist had tried to strangle her. Her small breasts were red and her nipples swollen and caked with dried blood. Out of modesty, Yasmeena opted not to inspect Lana's genital area, although she knew that the pooled blood indicated a substantial injury.

Yasmeena whispered, "Lana, what did he do to you?"

Lana did not explain, only moving her head slightly, and attempting to moisten her lips with her swollen tongue. "Thirsty," she said, her voice raspy and broken.

Yasmeena got up, looking around for water, finally finding two bottles of mineral water in the corner. She quickly did an inventory of the cell. There was nothing, other than Lana's mat, a chair, some ropes, the toilet, a pail for washing, and the two bottles of water. Lana had no food.

Once more she carefully cradled Lana's head, slowly releasing droplets of water into her mouth. It took long moments, but Lana slowly swallowed the contents of a bottle.

Yasmeena calculated the time she had before she must return to her own cell. The Captain had told her she could visit for only one hour. She pulled on the cords around Lana's wrists. They had been tightened until the cord had cut through the flesh to the bone. Regardless of the consequences she might face, Yasmeena worked on those cords until she untied Lana's arms and wrists. She tried to free Lana's bound ankles, but failed. She needed a sharp instrument to cut those cords. That was something she did not have.

"Thank you," Lana murmured. "My hands had become numb."

Yasmeena repeated, "Lana, what did he do to you?"

Lana's small body trembled. "The same...more of the same."

There was no need for further questions, as the truth was painfully obvious. Lana's rapist was still violently raping Lana as he always had, but the physical beatings were becoming more fierce. Lana looked as though she had been nearly beaten to death.

Despite her maimed physical condition, Lana was ravenous. She reported that she had not eaten for the past twenty-four hours. Her rapist had kept her tied anytime he was not raping her. He had set a new goal, Lana said, "He says he will break me down. He will force me to admit that I enjoy his attention. Never will I do that. I will die first."

Yasmeena cringed, feeling herself a coward, a woman manipulating the situation so that she might live. She knew that although Lana was a young girl, she was the strongest person she had ever known. She knew with certainty that Lana would never give in to her rapist. She would fight the beast so long as there was life.

Yasmeena concealed her sorrow and horror, carefully feeding the girl a pack of cookies and a few crackers. Lana then balanced the water bottle in her bloated hands and fingers, drinking what she could.

Yasmeena told her, "I have brought some medicine for pain, and some creams for your wounds. Can I help you apply them?"

"Please. Thank you. Please do help me."

Yasmeena wet a cloth in the water pail and gently cleaned the blood from Lana's face and upper chest. She paused at Lana's breasts, not certain what to do. She was embarrassed. Arab women by their nature and culture are extremely modest.

But by this time, Lana confided that she had been humiliated so many times by her rapist that she no longer felt shame for Yasmeena to see everything of her body. She told Yasmeena, "Go ahead, please do clean me, and apply the creams. Every part of my body is on fire and I can do nothing to help myself."

Without speaking, Yasmeena took her time, slowly, gently, cleaning the blood and the filth from Lana's body. Once she began to wash the young girl, Yasmeena realized that the filth was actually the rapist's semen. His semen was everywhere: In Lana's hair, on her face, the corners of her mouth, and on her chest. Lana's rapist was a monster and a wild man, spurting his evil semen all over the place. The Yasmeena of a few months ago would have been repulsed by such a thing, but now, she was strangely calm, wanting only to clean Lana, to get everything of the monster rapist off the Kuwaiti girl.

When Yasmeena paused once again at Lana's abdomen area, Lana said, "Do not be afraid. I want you to look. I want you to see what he has done to me."

111

Yasmeena became even more self-conscious. Never in her life had she looked closely at another woman's body. She had never really looked at her own body, and certainly had never inspected her genitals. All she needed to know was that she had genitals and that they were in their proper place between her legs. Yasmeena had never allowed herself to think about them as that area of a woman's body was considered taboo in her culture. She would even be ashamed to tell anyone that once after a particularly painful rape, she had touched her throbbing genitals, trying to figure out if there might be an infection between her legs.

Lana insisted. "No, please look. I cannot see what he has done, but I am hurting very badly between my legs, and I can feel that something is very grave down there."

Yasmeena glanced to see that Lana's ankles were tied apart, so her legs were spread wide. She moved slowly, worried about what she might see. When Yasmeena squatted between Lana's legs, Lana tried to open her thighs wider, but the ropes were too tight. Finally Lana scooted down, raising her legs slightly.

Yasmeena bit her lip to keep from inhaling. There was a strong stench although she could not actually see Lana's genitals. The tissue between Lana's legs was swollen to the size of a small melon, and colored bright blood red, resembling a huge tumor with blue veins growing out her body. The growth seemed to have a life of its own, and Yasmeena thought that she could see Lana's heartbeat in the swollen mass, as it seemed to throb with a certain cadence. The large pool of blood between Lana's legs was frightening.

Lana's eyes locked onto Yasmeena. "It is bad?"

"I do not know. I don't know what that area is supposed to look like."

"Is it bad?" Lana repeated, aware enough to know that Yasmeena was trying to spare her.

"Yes, Lana. It is bad," Yasmeena finally admitted. "You are very swollen. And you are very red and raw. I think you have an infection."

Lana nodded, her voice low and without toneless, as though she might be talking about something as mundane as going to the shopping mall. "I am sure that this beast who tortures me is not a human. He should be displayed to the public as a new and frightening species...in a cage. Listen to me, two days ago he visited a hospital and came back with some instruments that doctors use to open up women to examine them. He got excited about the idea of studying the female body, inside and out. He tied me in a position so that I could not struggle. Then he used those instruments on me, opening me up, then probing around for a long time with some other long medical gadgets that looked very dirty, crusted with blood and tissue. I begged him to stop, but he only became more aggressive with those instruments. I fear he has given me a serious infection with those things. I lost a lot of blood. Now everything down there has been throbbing for the last few hours."

"Oh, Lana. I am so sorry."

"Please. Put some of your medicine on it. And give me two of the pain pills."

Yasmeena could scarcely speak or move. Lana's situation was too ghastly to fathom, even as she was seeing it with her own eyes. Yasmeena wanted to run away, to bolt, to return to the amateur dramatics of her own cell, where nothing she did was real. Everything back there in Cell 15 was a performance. She was an actress playing a hated role; a critical role, but a role nevertheless, pretending to love the embraces of a sadistic rapist. The Captain was a man who knew nothing of his own reality, believing himself a king when he was nothing more than an uneducated poor man who thought the women he kidnapped and raped welcomed his sexual assaults. So his life was an act, too. In fact, Yasmeena's own rapes now seemed nearly routine, even dull, by comparison to Lana's reality. At the moment, she felt that to be ravished by the Captain was no more dangerous than a dip in the ocean while swimming steadily to avoid the sting of a jellyfish or the nip of an inquisitive baby shark.

In her heart Yasmeena felt that Lana would soon be dead. But now she fought against her panic, and moved to settle between Lana's legs, unscrewing the cap on the antibiotic cream. "This is going to hurt, Lana."

Lana smiled faintly, "I am accustomed to pain now."

But when Yasmeena's fingers brushed Lana's private area, Lana squirmed and squealed, unable to bear the slightest touch.

Yasmeena questioned how Lana would survive yet another rape before the day's end, for she knew that nothing would stop Lana's rapist from raping her...nothing. Yasmeena shivered when she considered what Lana would soon endure. Her monster rapist would soon rape her again, despite Lana's grave injuries. He would enjoy the young girl's agony.

"I must do this, Lana." Yasmeena looked around and plucked the empty water bottle from the floor. "Here, hold this, push it between your teeth. Try to bear this pain. It will help you."

Yasmeena heard the crunch of plastic as Lana bit down. She winced at Lana's soft moans as Yasmeena dabbed the entire tube on Lana's genitals. She looked around the room and found a few clean rags and wrapped those rags around Lana's bottom, holding everything tight with her hands until the bleeding subsided. Then she used the rags to mop up the blood.

Yasmeena then opened a second tube and began to apply the cream to Lana's nipples.

Suddenly there was a loud commotion. Yasmeena's heart sank when she saw the monster rapist charging at the cell door, roaring like a jungle lion, coming at them

114

both. He had unexpectedly returned to the prison for some reason.

Yasmeena sat without moving, as frozen as the ancient baby mammoth she had seen in a science magazine, terrified of the man who indeed resembled a beast more than a man.

Lana made little mewing sounds, like a kitten.

The two soldiers who had accompanied Yasmeena earlier now jumped into the fray, pulling the monster rapist by his arms, shouting at him, warning, *"Watch yourself!* Your Captain approved this visit!"

Yasmeena had never really taken a really close look at Lana's rapist until that moment. She saw that Lana was correct to nickname her rapist the Wolfman. This figure before Yasmeena appeared to be half man and half beast, a true Wolfman. This cruel creature belonged behind bars, a foul being that should be exhibited in a special traveling animal circus formed strictly to display bizarre beasts.

The beast was stronger than the two other rapists together. He broke free from their grasp, roughly grabbled Yasmeena by the arm, and pulled and then shoved her out of Lana's cell. Yasmeena saw him kicking the helpless Lana.

The two soldiers were alarmed, afraid that the beast might attack Yasmeena. They knew should that happen, the Captain would blame them. And so they hurried Yasmeena down the corridor and back to her cell, which suddenly seemed the calmest sanctuary in the world. Just as Yasmeena's cell door was closed and locked, Lana's anguished screams echoed throughout the entire prison.

With the image of what Lana was enduring flashing through in her mind, Yasmeena fell onto her mat. She felt as though every part of her body was weeping. She did not move for hours as a fog of despair oppressed her wholly.

Chapter Eleven: Survive!

Standoff in the Gulf
The day before the Security Council voted to authorize the use of force to evict Iraq from Kuwait after January 15, Kuwait made an unusual and moving presentation to the Council on human rights abuses committed by the Iraqi authorities. Using videotaped testimony and giant blowups of photos of torture victims, exiled Kuwaitis told a stunned and silent Security Council about the horrors they said Iraqi soldiers were inflicting on the Kuwaiti people. In its last report, Amnesty International said that based on scores of interviews with refugees, it had found a "horrifying picture of widespread arrests, torture under interrogation, summary executions, and mass extrajudicial killings."
—*The New York Times*
December 16, 1990

Yasmeena watched as a flash of anger quickly passed over the Captain's face. Then he controlled his anger, although his lips still puckered with irritation. He had just learned about the altercation between Lana's rapist and the other soldiers. Yasmeena felt a burden lifted to know that the Captain was displeased with Lana's rapist, and not with her, for one never knew how the Captain might react to unanticipated circumstances. She was also concerned that Lana might be blamed. The Captain had made it clear more than once that Lana's shrieks and wails irritated him, giving Yasmeena the impression that he was hopeful that Lana's rapist would tire of the hysterical girl and have her shot. But thus far the beastly rapist remained enamored of Lana, her cries and anguish exciting him as he seemingly savored his full ownership of the beautiful young girl. The beast wanted Lana alive to be raped.

Yasmeena sat silent for an hour as the Captain sat and stared at the new ceiling fan in Yasmeena's cell as though the fan had some important secret to reveal.

Yasmeena hoped the Captain would finally punish the beast. If wishes could come true, she wanted him to be so angry that he would transfer Lana's rapist to another unit. Or perhaps command him to stop torturing the girl. Not that every girl raped was not being tortured, but Lana's torture compared to their own was like comparing Mt. Everest to a small hill in northern Lebanon. Lana's rapist appeared committed to brutalizing his young victim to the edge of death.

Yasmeena thought the brute had been trained in torture. He mechanically produced the most excruciating pain without causing death, a skill only expert torturers had mastered.

Yasmeena had heard about similar persistent torture. Her knowledge came from knowing a family whose two sons had accidently crossed the border from Lebanon into Syria while hunting birds near the village of Jazzin. The boys were still youthful, the youngest only eighteen and the oldest not yet twenty-one. They were arrested and transported to Damascus where they were charged as spies. The eldest of the two boys was executed in front of his brother within a month of the arrest, and the survivor was ruthlessly tortured for two years. Then out of the blue sky, and without explanation, the Syrians brought him to the border of Lebanon and threw him from an automobile, ordering him to get to his village and warn all he knew not to spy against Syria.

When kidnapped, he was a young and healthy man; two years later, he returned an aged and broken man, telling his dismayed parents about the death of their oldest son, and horrifying them with the tales of his torture. To all who listened, such brutality and persecution seemed scarcely plausible. But his audience knew of the cruel Assad Baathist regime in Syria. And, the victim was well known to be exceedingly straightforward, while the boy's appearance alone argued for the truth of his story.

Of course, the village women were not told the particulars, for Arab men exclude women from such conversations. However, Yasmeena had overheard her father tell his brother that he was glad to have daughters if only because their unstable Middle Eastern world was too dangerous for young men. Yasmeena was intrigued by his statement. She knew that her mother's greatest sorrow in life was not providing her husband with a son and now she was overhearing her father emphatically state that he was happy *not* to be the father of a son.

When she overheard men discussing the fate of the neighbor's son, she was drawn to the conversation, and so she listened. Later she regretted her curiosity for she had not known of such things before. She could never again look at the neighbor's son in the same normal way. Now she imagined him naked and forced to sit on a sharp metal object that tore open his rectum and ripped his intestines, or hanging from a ceiling fan while electrodes were attached to his genitals.

With both Syria and Iraq governed by Baathist regimes, she now assumed that there was something particularly vile about the Baathist method of ruling.

She could say little to her Captain because her position as a rape victim was that of an obedient servant and lover. The Captain was not a man who would accept the opinion of a woman. While her thoughts were abuzz with the things the Captain might do to save all the women, she remained silent, not wanting to derail her own advancing situation. She stirred in the small cell, serving hot tea to the Captain while he waited for her to boil a few eggs on the hotplate. She took the yogurt out of her small refrigerator and very carefully placed the food exactly as the Captain liked it: Shelled and boiled eggs in the middle, two spoons of yogurt on the side, with fresh pita bread wrapped in a clean cloth. If the Captain could find any fruit in the market, he liked to complete his meal with fruit, although the longer the occupation, the more difficult it was to find fruit in the markets, according to the soldiers in charge of stealing the food.

He finally stopped gazing at the ceiling fan and began to eat, his movements hurried, a man hungry. Yasmeena once again sat quietly, waiting for him to finish his meal. She knew that she would have plenty of time to eat later, after the Captain had raped her for a few hours.

She sat thinking, but said nothing. The Captain was not a man to encourage polite conversation while eating. Remembering her educated father and how carefully he selected items from his plate, to chew quietly while he talked with his wife and children about social matters, Yasmeena compared the Captain's rough manners and found him sorely lacking.

After wiping the remains of the egg with the pita bread, the Captain looked at Yasmeena and ordered, "Take everything off and get on your stomach."

She did, and he glutted himself as he leisurely raped her from the back, and she professed pleasure, even as she gritted her teeth. But she was very happy she was being raped by the Captain rather than by Lana's monster rapist. She thanked God for that small favor. Later she forced herself to smile pleasantly and tell the Captain how good it was and even pleaded for him not to leave, but to stay and keep her company. Her talent for manipulating the Captain was improving. She told him the biggest lie when she said, "I miss you when you are not here."

He smiled, a little, not surprised that Yasmeena had fallen in love with him. He then washed up and

119

dressed. At the cell door he turned back and stared at her. Finally he spoke, dragging out his words as though he had all day just to utter a few words. "You have my permission to continue visiting the girl once each day. You can visit at five o'clock each afternoon, but only for one hour. I will tell my men."

Seeing her worried look, he could read her mind. "You will not be disturbed again. He will be told that is your time."

Yasmeena found the courage to ask, "But what if he becomes so angry he kills her?"

The Captain shrugged, "That is not my business. The girl is his. He can do with her as he likes. It is my business if he defies my order that you are to visit the girl." He paused, "If he touches you again, he will regret it."

That's when Yasmeena knew that in many ways her Captain was more dangerous than the beast. The beast was ruled by emotion, and was only a danger to the women he raped. The Captain was unfeeling, and could easily kill anyone if they challenged him.

Yasmeena was once again reminded of the frightening reality that she was safe only as long as she pleased him. She could make no mistakes. Her Captain, the man who thought he might love her, the man who was convinced that she loved him, the man who was thinking of making her his second wife, could turn into a killer instantly should she disappoint him.

That was not going to happen. Since the moment she had made the choice to live, she had become exactly the woman the Captain desired. And that is the only reason Yasmeena would live.

Chapter Twelve: You Can Never Go Home Again

The UN Security Council set a deadline of January 15, 1991, for a complete Iraqi withdrawal from Kuwait. Rather than leave, Saddam dug in and exhorted his soldiers and his people to prepare for the "mother of all battles" that was soon to come.

—*Understanding Iraq*
Joseph Tragert

Yasmeena thought that Lana looked like a child despite the fact she was dressed in a woman's sheer black negligée. Obviously this was one of the items the monster rapist had stolen and forced her to wear. But at least Lana was no longer naked with her wrists and ankles bound. She was lying quietly on her mat, with her back to the cell door. She visibly trembled when the cell door opened, doubtless fearing that her rapist had unexpectedly returned once more.

"It is Yasmeena, Lana," Yasmeena said softly. "There is no reason to be afraid."

"Yasmeena. No. No. Please, Yasmeena, you must stay away," Lana appealed. "He promised to kill us both."

Backed by certainty that her Captain would protect her, Yasmeena was willing to take the chance. "Then we die together, Lana," she said assuredly. Yasmeena had good reason for confidence as she had been told an important secret. The Captain did not dally in letting the monster know that he was displeased. Around the time of noon, her Captain had volunteered Lana's rapist to the area commander who needed a soldier to deliver some documents to the Saudi border area. Yasmeena knew the Captain was angry with the man, and this was his way to show his displeasure, to keep him from having sex for a day.

"Let's not worry, Lana. I have been told that the monster is on a military mission and he will not return until tomorrow. You are safe for this night, at least."

Lana inhaled loudly as she slowly turned over, hopeful surprise on her face. Yasmeena assumed that the poor dear was thinking that for the first time since she was kidnapped, she would only be raped once in the day, rather than the rapist's carefully timed three rapes every twenty-four hours. Although Lana appeared exhausted and near death, Yasmeena saw cautious optimism began to glow in the young girl's eyes.

Yasmeena smiled, and Lana attempted to smile, but her face was so swollen and bruised that she could do little more than contort her severely ravaged features.

Yasmeena was horrified but didn't react. She would concentrate on their good fortune. In fact, she was carrying several bags filled with water, milk, some fruit, a grilled chicken, two slices of pita bread, and even a Turkish sweet covered in honey, something the Captain had bought for Yasmeena, but she would give to Lana. Actually, she had eaten lightly for the past twenty-four hours to save most of her food for Lana. She laid the packages on the floor and turned to Lana, sitting beside her, lightly touching her on the shoulder. She reached for Lana's hand, but pulled back at the last moment after seeing that Lana's fingers were swollen, bloody, and grossly misshapen.

Lana's broken digits triggered in Yasmeena's mind the image of an old familiar face. She was remembering her favorite of the family's former drivers. The poor man was a good person, always gentle and kind to everyone, taking special pleasure from children since he saw his own children only once every two years, when he left Lebanon for a month's paid leave. He was from Sri Lanka and had left his family there to seek work in the Middle East. The poor man's fingers were a source of enormous curiosity for all the children in the neighborhood, for each of his fingers was appallingly mutilated, some cut off at the knuckles, some bent downward, and others twisted upward, each seemingly turned in a different direction. That kind man had chuckled at his misfortune, telling the nosy kids that when a child he had been too curious about things that were not his concern. And so it happened that his hands had been caught in a machine in his uncle's machinery shop.

Yasmeena thought it was a miracle that he could use those hands to drive an automobile, but he had assured her and the other children that fingers pointed in all directions proved an asset for a driver. He held out those fingers, joking with the children that, "When I need to turn the wheel of the car, my brain connects with the correct finger, which steers perfectly and off we go in the proper direction!"

Yasmeena shook her head to clear the image from her mind. Her mouth was dry and she could barely speak, but she found the words to ask, "Lana, darling girl, tell me, what did he do to your hands?"

"Oh, my hands," Lana said in a dreamy voice, raising her arms and looking at her hands and fingers carefully, as if she was seeing them for the first time. "Oh, he asked if I played a musical instrument. I told him not really, but that I had always wanted to play the piano. He looked at me for the longest time, grinning his evil smile. He said, no, that is not going to happen. I had no idea what he meant, and forgot it, to tell you the truth. But later in the day after raping me for an hour or so, he bound me with ropes like I was an animal. Once it was impossible for me to move a muscle, he began laughing like a hyena dog. Before I knew what was in his sick mind, he squatted beside me and pressed my arms down with his knees, holding one hand down and then the other. He beat my fingers against the hard floor with a hammer."

Lana stared at her fingers once again. "I think he broke all the bones," she mused mildly. She frowned as she held out her arms, giving Yasmeena a good look at her fingers. "What do you think? Don't you think all these bones are broken?"

"Oh, Lana," Yasmeena whispered.

"It is okay. I will never get to play a piano, anyway. You, and I, know that he is going to kill me."

"Don't say that, Lana."

Lana shrugged. "We know the truth. I am going to die here."

Yasmeena fought a stinging rush of resignation, knowing that despite the odds, she must use all her power to save Lana. She had grown to love her as dearly as she loved her three sisters. She must instill hope in the young girl, who was rapidly losing faith that she might live. "Lana, you can do this, Inshallah. You can outlast this brute. My Captain says that I can come to you every day. He has given me permission to bring you some nourishing food. We will build up your strength." She repeated with emphasis, as though to give Lana the courage and determination she needed, "You can make the choice to live. Only then will you outlast this brute."

Then Yasmeena stood up and leaned against the cell bars, being certain the soldiers were not listening, before returning to whisper in Lana's ear. "Listen, Lana, listen. My Captain is worried. He allowed me to have a radio, although I cannot listen unless he is with me. He and I sometimes listen to the BBC. The Americans and British governments say that they are coming into Kuwait, and that they are going to force the Iraqi army to leave Kuwait. A huge army has built up in Saudi Arabia after King Fah'd agreed for them use to the country as the base for this big fight. The radio says that many other countries have joined the Western armies, even Middle Eastern countries that disagree with Saddam's actions.

"My Captain is genuinely worried for the first time. He thinks there will be a big battle but that Iraq cannot defeat everyone. He is hoping that Saddam will order them to leave Kuwait. If that happens, you and I will be free, and this nightmare will end. It will end, Lana; it will end."

Lana grimaced sweetly, an affectionate look in her eyes. "Oh, Yasmeena, I do so hope you live. I do. You have been a saint to all the girls here. But look at me. I am destroyed. How can I return to my family like this?"

Yasmeena was dazed into stillness. She didn't move. She stared without speaking, for she had suffered the same doubts and fears, and now her misgivings and anxieties assailed her once again, only with a greater force than before. Yasmeena knew that she would never reveal the truth to her family, that she had been kidnapped and held captive and raped. Although her parents loved her, their happiness would be destroyed by the knowledge that their eldest and most beautiful daughter was damaged goods. It would be impossible for Yasmeena to marry. There would be gossip about her, and that gossip would be an invisible scandal wrapped around the entire family. They would all be shunned by good society.

Such reactions were common in the Middle East. Any girl raped would be blamed for her rape. It was the girl's responsibility to remain pure. Yasmeena would be blamed for flying into Kuwait. Yasmeena would be blamed for leaving her friends to stay in a Kuwaiti home. Yasmeena would be blamed for helping the Kuwaiti fighters by transporting handbills. Yasmeena would be blamed for driving the car. Yasmeena would be blamed for being at the roadblock. But most of all, Yasmeena would be blamed for surviving.

Even if she remained alive and returned to her family and her country, and even if she could find the strength to endure the end of all good things in her life, she could never ever reveal that she had made the choice to play a deadly game with her rapist, a game where she pretended to care about him, or to enjoy his forced rapes. If she should admit such a thing, even her mother and father would turn away. At the very least, her family and society would expect her to fight her rapist every moment of every day.

Because of the actions she had taken to survive, Yasmeena would be forever reviled. Yasmeena would never again be respected by anyone, even if she outwitted her wicked Captain and lived to tell the tale of the prison circus, the house of rape. When it came to rape, life itself was considered unimportant. A woman's honor was the only thing that really mattered. Honor was the gauge of respect.

In truth, Yasmeena's family would expect her to behave like Lana, a woman who never ever gave in.

Lana might be beaten to death, or shot by her rapist, but even in death, she would keep something even more important than life...Lana would be buried with her honor intact. She would have respect from her family, community and culture, respect that she had never given in, respect that she had chosen honor over life.

Comparing herself to the courageous Lana, Yasmeena felt a rush of shame as strong as a 100-mile-an-hour wind. Surely, she was the lowest of creatures, a fallen woman who said false words to her rapist, a woman who feigned pleasure while being fucked by a man she had not wed, a woman who would do anything to survive, when in fact her family would rather bury her than to accept her embraces of a man not her husband.

At that moment, Yasmeena felt the disgrace of every moment she had endured with her Captain. For the first time, Yasmeena knew that she could never go home again.

Chapter Thirteen: Tick, Tick, Tick: From Midnight to Dawn

After ministering medications to Lana and coaxing her to eat bits of chicken wrapped in pita bread, Yasmeena hid the remaining food under one of the three fancy nightgowns still folded in a box stacked in a corner of the cell. Lana had mentioned that for some reason the beast never looked through her clothing, although he frequently rummaged through everything else in the cell, looking for something to spark the long-standing rage that permanently simmered in his heart.

Yasmeena had planned a nice long chat with Lana, to tell her all the exciting details she had learned of the military buildup in Saudi Arabia, the only event that gave her hope their nightmare would end one day, and that the day might be soon. But Lana was nearly immobilized in pain from her mangled fingers. The poor girl could scarcely follow their conversation.

Rather than strain Lana with talk, Yasmeena consoled her friend with her calming presence, patting her on the shoulders and soothing her forehead with her fingers, and finally making an effort to comb out the tangles of Lana's long hair with her fingers. Lana was blessed with waves of beautiful black hair that hung to her waist.

Lana had previously confided that she had always been proud of her hair, so thick that her mother and sisters exclaimed over its beauty, declaring it a perfect frame for a flawless face. In the beginning of her imprisonment, she had endeavored to keep her hair in one thick braid, but after the beast used her hair as a weapon-- seeming to take pleasure from throwing her around the room by her plait--she stopped that practice. After the beast wrapped it her neck and choked her with it until she passed out, Lana longed for a pair of scissors so that she might cut her prized hair into a bob.

But none of the women were permitted to possess such an item. Even Lana's Captain would not allow her to acquire a sharp instrument. Those who victimize, brutalize and terrorize must always fear uprisings.

Suddenly Lana noticed something unusual about Yasmeena. Yasmeena was wearing a diamond encrusted gold Rolex watch, one of several extravagant items the Captain had found on the sidewalk outside one of Kuwait City's most illustrious jewelry stores. The previous thieves had evidently overstuffed their bags with dazzling watches and jewels, spilling the overflow as they ran away. The Captain just happened by as thieves were running and these jewels lay like treasure at his feet.

He had scooped them up and told no one but Yasmeena, because soldiers were supposed to send everything of value back to the palaces of Saddam, so that the dictator and his family could keep all Kuwaiti wealth. Since the Captain had plans to make Yasmeena his second wife, he had elected to present her with the smallest of the watches. He was pompous when boasting to Yasmeena that he was saving two of the watches for his mother and his wife back in Iraq. The final two he would keep for other wives, should he take a third or fourth.

With the stolen wealth of Kuwait boosting his financial worth, the Captain was dreaming big dreams. He had worked diligently in Kuwait to gain the attention of his superior, who now depended upon him for many small tasks. He was now counting on a promotion. He mused that perhaps the days of poverty were behind him and if only Iraq could hold Kuwait, he felt certain he would be promoted to a ruling position in the 19th province. He saw the possibility of one day becoming a respected sheik in his small village, building four villas that would be occupied with four wives. He bragged to Yasmeena, "I will finally get the life I deserve. I will keep my first wife out of respect; after all, she is the mother of my first born-son. But I will fill the other three villas with young and glamorous women." Then he would spend the rest of his days fucking women so beautiful that he would be the envy of his friends. He laughed loudly at the image, heaving back his head and opening his mouth so wide that Yasmeena could see his entire tongue and even into his gullet which looked bright red, as though highlighted by fire. Surely, she thought, hell was in this man's innards.

Yasmeena had nearly choked with fury when he presented her with the watch. These rapists thought they could quiet their captives with trinkets, but even expensive trinkets could not buy her love. The Captain was happier than he had been since she met him, as he revealed his plans for a harem. Despite her anger, she successfully struggled to keep her acting fresh and persuasive. She exclaimed with delight, making him believe that her only dream in life was to be his wife and to receive his big thing every chance she got. The truth was that if she ever got the opportunity, she would cut his appendage from his body and nail it to a stake and let it sizzle and shrivel in the hot sun. Or perhaps she would fry it in hot oil. There were a host of things she might do to bring herself a measure of justice. But for the time being, she fought back those emotions and wore the flawless watch with an equally flawless smile on her face.

Yasmeena was a commonsense kind of a girl, and told herself that she would settle accounts later–with the Captain and with her own soul. This deception with the Captain was costing Yasmeena her self-respect. But she brushed aside such thoughts, thinking that the watch might come in handy later. Perhaps if something happened to the Captain, she could barter the expensive watch for her life, and for Lana's life.

Lana suddenly noticed the gold Rolex, mentioning, "Mommy has a similar watch. My father gave it to her for their wedding anniversary last year." Lana's brow knitted in thought, but Yasmeena blushed in shame when she understood that her friend was too kindhearted to ask Yasmeena how it was that such a costly item was clasped around her wrist.

Yasmeena withdrew her arm, knowing that if Lana had been offered such a watch she would have smashed it and thrown it in her rapist's face. Yet Yasmeena calmed her anguish by reminding herself that she had worn the watch when visiting Lana for a practical reason: she must not overstay her allotted visiting hour.

But once Lana saw the watch, the visit was spoiled because Lana could think of nothing but time, repeatedly asking how many hours she had before the beast appeared from his journey. Did Yasmeena think he would return in time for the morning rape? Lana's life was now ruled by the three daily rapes. For certain, whatever time the beast might return, it would be too soon.

Yasmeena's scheduled visit with Lana passed more rapidly than she wanted. She would have liked to stay with her friend forever, to protect her from the beast. But the watch told the sad tale, that the time had come for Lana to be alone to face her fears of what was ahead of her, whether in the morning or in the afternoon. Yasmeena could do nothing to keep Lana from being raped and tortured. She could only visit once daily and do her best to offer some small comfort.

Worried about Lana's physical decline, a reluctant Yasmeena hugged her friend goodbye for the day, telling her that she would return the following afternoon.

The two women stared intently at each other, neither wanting to break their spiritual connection. Neither could speak the unspeakable, although Yasmeena whispered the unthinkable, words she had never intended to say. "Lana, can you let him have his way without fighting? Can you go along with him? Can you pretend? Is this possible?"

Lana gazed at Yasmeena with a perceptive expression, and it was clear at that moment that she fully comprehended Yasmeena's conspiracy to outmaneuver her Captain. Yet there was no reproach in her manner, for Lana was a generous spirit and thought no less of Yasmeena for her deceptive charade. She then spoke with a sweetness that tugged at Yasmeena's heart. "No. I cannot. It is impossible. I will fight him until I am free, or until he kills me." Lana smiled faintly, "But someone must live, Yasmeena. Someone must tell what has happened here. One of these days I will be shot. One of these days they will fling this broken body into an unmarked grave. This is my fate. My parents must not then waste their lives looking for me. They will need a mourning time, and then go on living for their other children. I am relieved that you will live on."

Yasmeena nodded meekly, too abashed to speak. She knew in her heart that Lana deserved to live a full life, but that she would not.

"Listen Yasmeena, your survival will help my family. Try to find a paper and a writing instrument. When the time draws near to war, I must give you information. You must know my family name and the location of our home. Until now, I have told no one, too fearful that the beast will go after my mother and sisters. But after this is over, I want you to contact them. They must know that I am dead. You must tell them that my honor was stolen from me, but that I never stopped fighting, and that I chose death over life. They will understand."

After a heartfelt embrace, a shamefaced Yasmeena stumbled from Lana's cell, returning to her own, feeling herself to be the most reprehensible woman who had ever lived. At that moment, she would have stepped in front of bullets meant for Lana, for Yasmeena had persuaded herself that while Lana was worthy of life, she was not.

From that evening, Yasmeena's total concentration was to help Lana. She most wanted to save her life, but if she failed, and the beast murdered Lana, then Yasmeena must carry out her friend's wishes. She must convince her Captain to provide her some paper and a pen. She felt confident that she could get him to do her bidding, for with every passing day, her deception was becoming more credible. The Captain was like a spoiled child, easy to sway so long as he was getting exactly what he wanted.

Yasmeena knew the man well by this time, and his absolute self-assurance that he was a man like no other--a handsome desirable man to whom even a rape victim would lose their heart--would have been absurd under any other circumstances. The truth was that the Captain was not handsome, or charming, or kindly. He was ordinary in the most monotonous sense of the word. God had given him a characterless visage, and his body was no improvement over his face. He was tall and lanky with a round paunch, entirely unremarkable when it came to his physique. While he was not physically disgusting as was Lana's rapist, he was bland, the kind of man who would bore a bride before the honeymoon ended. While he seemed to have some intelligence when it came to military matters and in leading soldiers, in all other ways, he was a man afflicted with the most tedious drabness.

Had the Captain ever been an airline passenger in Yasmeena's section, the memory of his face would have faded before the food tray cart passed his seat.

Yasmeena fretted. Surely she was clever enough to get paper and pen from this man. Before the Captain arrived for a rape and a meal, Yasmeena had polished her plan.

On this night he startled her when he burst into the cell door an insatiable rapist. Caught unawares, Yasmeena had to work diligently to keep up the masquerade. Without taking a moment to ask her about her day, or to tell her about his day, the Captain order, "Strip! Quickly! I am uncomfortable." He rubbed his hands over his penis. "Hurry! I must do it quickly or I might become ill!"

Yasmeena concealed her distaste, disrobing hastily. Before she could slip out of her panties, the Captain was naked and on top of her. The Captain ripped her panties into three pieces when he tore them from her body. Still, she feigned pleasure while he raped her from the front, and then from the back. But still he did not orgasm, so once again he went back inside her, pumping away, then stopped, telling her that he must put it in that special place in the back. He had been thinking about the time he did it and about how tight she was in there.

Yasmeena's entire body quivered. She could never forget the physical damage she had suffered the one time he had subjected her to that kind of rape, but before she could say a word to remind him that she had believed she was safe from such painful sex, he flipped her onto her stomach. The Captain stood and she heard him rummage around in her cosmetics bag. He returned with a jar of her face cream. She lay there helpless while he took his fingers and with the cream swabbed out that private place. He seemed to enjoy the effect of seeing her squirm because she hated his dirty fingers inside her and because the cream burned the delicate membranes inside her like a flame of fire. "This will help you, sweetie," he said, in a sugary tuneful voice unlike any he had ever used before. "This will keep my big thing from hurting you."

Then he grabbed her small body and pulled her up by her hips and before she could plead with him not to hurt her, he was in, thrusting as hard as he could.

The pain of anal sex was as acute as she remembered. Yasmeena crammed a fist into her mouth to keep from shrieking, because she knew that her Captain bragged that she welcomed his embraces and his every touch, and he would become furious if his men heard her begging him to stop.

He did orgasm quickly, but she could feel warm blood mingling with his semen as it rolled down the back of her legs and onto her thighs.

Afterward he hugged her from behind and whispered, "See. It is better than you remembered. It is best that we will do this every day so that I can stretch you out. You will come to love it."

The Captain was in such a good mood that he stayed longer than usual, quietly confiding in Yasmeena everything he had heard about the Allied military buildup amassing in Saudi Arabia. It seemed that their enemies were afraid of Saddam's armies, for they were gathering a huge fighting force. With an odd smile on his face he told her that the Iraqi army was also preparing for full war. They had no other choice. Saddam would never give in, so it would be a fight to the death.

Yasmeena quaked in fear. The last thing she wanted was to be locked in a prison cell while bombs were falling. She had heard enough about that kind of terrifying violence from friends and relatives who were stuck in apartments in Beirut during the 1982 Israeli assault upon Lebanon.

When the Captain saw Yasmeena's worried expression, he petted her by rubbing her shoulders and saying, "Do not worry sweetie. I will not let anything happen to you. I will think of something," he promised.

The Captain felt so amiable toward Yasmeena that when she mentioned she wanted to spend her lonely hours making sketches, perhaps even to sketch his handsome face, but that she required drawing paper and some colored pencils, he grinned like the fool he was. "You will have it, my little ducky, my little wife."

Yasmeena did as she was told when he leaned in, whispering that he desired her yet again. She paid a great penalty for his agreement to those artist supplies when he grew aroused yet again and insisted on a precise repetition of the earlier rape.

When the Captain finally left her alone in her cell, Yasmeena collapsed on her mat and wept, sensing for the first time in a week that she, too, would perish along with Lana. Her small body could not withstand such brutal attacks on a daily basis. How long could she imitate pleasure at being raped so brutally and painfully?

With sadness hovering like those thick black clouds that often circle over the mountains of Lebanon to plunge a sunny day into darkness, Yasmeena squeezed her eyes shut, giving herself over to the vision that haunted her when she was at her gloomiest. She sat quietly, reflecting on the insistent horror of a violent death and the pain she knew would pierce her body when the day arrived that she was tied to a stake and before unfeeling men grasping powerful weapons. She decided she would not close her eyes at that moment, but would instead glimpse the deadly metal bullets that would spit from the lethal weapons to enter her small body and end her life.

The image was nearly more than she could bear. She did not want to die. She wanted to live. Yasmeena shivered and cried but fought to regain her mental strength. She reminded herself that she was a strong woman and she *would not, she could not* allow the Captain, a man who was nothing more than a criminal rapist, to cut her young life short.

Yasmeena held her head in her hands, and shaking with determination, told herself that she would live!

She wanted to live! She must live!

Chapter Fourteen: Until Basra!

War in the Gulf:
Allied air power continued to pound Iraqi troop positions today while artillery and tank fire echoed across the Kuwaiti border, but there was no sign of further Iraqi movements into Saudi Arabia
—*The New York Times*
February 2, 1991

War in the Gulf:
Allied fighter-bombers pounded enemy troop emplacements in every corner of Kuwait today, flying a record number of missions over the emirate despite clouds of inky smoke from oil-well fires, apparently set by Iraqi, that covered a quarter of the nation.
—*The New York Times*
February 23, 1991

Radio Baghdad & Al Shabbab TV Station (Owned by Uday Hussein)
"Iraqi troops are starting their harvest of the necks of the infidel, corrupt and impudent aggressors in the epic of the mother of battles."
—President Saddam Hussein
February 25, 1991

Al Thawra (Revolution) in Baghdad
Iraqi readers enjoyed various cartoons published in Iraqi newspapers today.

One cartoon showed American soldiers in coffins with the coffins stamped with the word "Export."
Another cartoon pictured an American soldier marching into Iraq as a skeleton.
—*Al Thawra newspaper*
February 25, 1991

January 17, 1991

Yasmeena was confused. Was the day gone? Had the night come? From Yasmeena's cell she could see no outdoor light. Only the Captain's coming and going told the time. He told her that the day was January 17, 1990 and the Allied armies had started their air war. He had to go and report to his superior, but he would return. Shortly after he left her cell, Yasmeena heard the distant, rolling, rumbling, threatening, all-encompassing sound of bombs.

Her heart pounding, Yasmeena listened. The war had finally started. Her fright was cloaked by hope and promise of salvation. Although Yasmeena feared that she would survive her rapist only to die under the Allied bombs, she knew that it would take full war to convince the Iraqi dictator to release his grasp of Kuwait. She would have to endure the terror and use her wits to survive.

Her fear slowly eased when Kuwait City was mainly spared. She breathed a little easier, grateful that their future liberators were taking care not to bomb areas they knew were populated by civilians.

There was another, more serious concern. Yasmeena believed that before they were routed from the city, the rapists would execute their prisoners.

February 4, 1991

Everything was coming from the clouds as bombs continued to fall in the distance, day after day. There was no sign of an invading army. While the rape victims were frequently terrified into tears, the rapists still swaggered, boasting to the girls that they would soon see something unexpected: American and British soldiers occupying a few cells. They were confident that they would destroy the enemy and end up with many new prisoners. They had special plans for those soldiers, too, which included the dreaded acid baths, a favorite kind of torture they had been perfecting against the Kuwaiti freedom fighters. Those acid baths always terrified the most courageous of men. It was a simple way of killing a man. Fill a vat with acid and hoist the enemy naked above the deadly potion. Sometimes they extended the torture, letting the enemy hang there and think about how painful death was going to be. Death did not come from a simple drop into the acid. No, they would lower the victim slowly, letting the acid work on the feet and then the legs and then the body. Generally the victim didn't stop screaming for mercy until his head went under the acid. Seeing a man's flesh burned off his bones was a shocking sight.

Sometimes they would add to the fun and toss one of the Kuwaitis' pet dogs or cats into the vat first. The dog howls and the cat screeches sometimes caused the watching victim to lose control of his bowels. But the shit fell into the vat so there was no need for bystanders to worry about being covered in Kuwaiti shit.

Yes, they bragged, they would teach their enemies not to underestimate Saddam Hussein.

Overhearing such explicit threats brought Yasmeena to the realization that being raped was not the worst thing that could happen to her. In fact, she didn't know whether to be worried or excited. Her fondest dream was to see the last of the Captain and every Iraqi soldier. Such a thought brought a smile. But she didn't want to be executed as the Iraqis were withdrawing. That possibility produced a pained grimace.

Her Captain was worried, too. He had more military awareness than his men, and he had confided to Yasmeena that Saddam's army would be no match for what was coming at them from across the desert. He was privy to information not available to low-ranking soldiers. He knew that their enemies had gathered a huge army and wielded the latest technology. They intended to win this war. Saddam's gamble had not paid off. Nearly the whole world had joined together to pressure him through the United Nations. The Iraqis would leave Kuwait, of that the Captain was sure. But he knew that Saddam would delay the withdrawal to the last hour because Saddam always expected miracles to save him when he had miscalculated.

At this point, the Captain didn't care much about Saddam or anyone else. For the first time, he criticized the Iraqi dictator, lowering his voice to say, "Saddam and his tribe sit in Baghdad and consume the oil wealth as though they had pissed it from their loins, rather than admit that Iraqi oil formed in the earth beneath the feet of the Iraqis."

Instantly he seemed to regret his words. He sucked in his breath and pursed his lips, knowing that Iraqis who expressed anything other than total devotion and worship for Saddam endangered their entire family. From the days of his youth, he had paid homage to Saddam Hussein.

"Saddam is not the point," he muttered. His only goal was to survive. He would save Yasmeena, too, he promised.

February 25, 1991

After more than a month of constant bombing around the perimeter of Kuwait City, the end felt near. What else was there left to bomb? Kuwait was a small country. Soon the Allied tanks and soldiers would arrive, Yasmeena felt certain. Earlier in the day her Captain told her that he and his men were waiting for orders from Baghdad telling them what they should do.

Yasmeena wanted to be physically strong when liberation came, so she was eating more than usual and taking regular naps. Around three in the afternoon on February 25th, Yasmeena was sleeping. But her sleep was not restful. She tossed and turned before drifting back into a troubled sleep.

She suffered terrifying nightmares so convincing that she was certain the dreams were reality. In her nightmare she was wedged in a tunnel of dark dreams, one passageway following the other like an endless film loop unfolding many disturbing scenes. Yasmeena witnessed the brutal murder of her parents, their eyes protruding in disbelief as they gaped from their daughter to the Captain, who pointed a fearsome weapon at their torsos. Yasmeena breathlessly watched, mouth open in a silent scream as the Captain's trigger finger squeezed and her parents crumbled to the ground in unbearably slow motion. Then she caught a glimpse of Lana's nude corpse as she was pulled rigid and cold from her cell. So! Lana's greatest fear had been realized. She did not survive the prison circus. The most alarming image came to her when the Captain arrived in Yasmeena's cell to boast that he had just completed an inventive course on how to read minds. Just looking at her he could enter her innermost thoughts. And so with his new power he easily detected her deception. He suddenly knew that the woman he trusted and pampered, the woman who had eagerly accepted his treasured embraces, did not love him. He was enraged to discover that she loathed him, that she filled many hours plotting his dismemberment and murder.

In a quiet fury her Captain convened a trial. The judges were the raping guards. She was reassured to hear that her punishment was not going to be death, until the

141

verdict was announced: She was to be given to Lana's rapist to do with as he pleased.

As the leering beast reached out to claim her, a series of loud noises jolted Yasmeena out of the nightmare. What was that thunderous clamor? For a small and lovely moment she believed herself to be in a posh hotel in Beirut overlooking the Mediterranean, celebrating New Year's Eve fireworks with family and friends. As Yasmeena's mind stumbled from its bleary haze her heart fluttered. Those popping noises were not fireworks but were gunshots! Was she hearing the execution of one of the prison victims? If so, which of the girls was being murdered? Lana! Was it Lana? Had the beast finally killed that sweet girl?

Before Yasmeena could move, the entire prison was jolted into acute chaos. Loud footsteps could be heard throughout the prison. Shouting guards appeared to be running in one direction and returning in another. The pleas and screams of women suddenly erupted, the building quickly filling with shrieks and cries so loud that Yasmeena conjured the image of the flat roof blowing off the prison.

What was going on?

Yasmeena disregarded her aches and pains from the previous night's rapes and pushed with her hands to stand on her feet. She pulled the first dress her fingers touched over her head and slipped her feet into a pair of sandals. Something significant was happening. She switched to automatic pilot, seizing a small bag and tossing in a few bottles of water and some pieces of pita bread and various snack foods.

The dulled sense of danger had never left her. Was this the day she would die? Had her nightmare been a premonition, a preparation of what was to come? Had the Americans and the British and the Saudis and the Syrians and all the armies that had been gathering in Saudi Arabia

142

made a surprise strike? Would such a military attack trigger a massacre at the prison?

She had never forgotten her Captain's direst warning from the early days of her imprisonment. He had said that if Iraqi forces in Kuwait were attacked, they were ordered to leave no witnesses to any crimes. Certainly no rape victims would be left alive to attest to crimes. Without living witnesses, the soldiers could refute their ugly addiction of seizing virginal women for raping fun. The Captain later assured Yasmeena that while she would not be harmed, all the other women would be executed.

Yasmeena listened carefully for the sound of distant gunfire. There was none. Surely an attacking army pouring into Kuwait City would create a loud commotion. Still, there was no denying that the prison guards were preparing for *something* big.

She braced herself for the moment that had finally come. She knew more than most people trapped in Kuwait knew only because her Captain had told her what Iraqi military plans he knew. After listening to the reports he would sit quietly, telling her not to interrupt, that he must consider the soundest plan for their survival. The Captain knew that change was coming, and that perhaps Iraq would not be able to keep Kadhima, their 19th province. Perhaps it would be necessary to redraw world maps for Iraqi schoolchildren so that Kuwait would exist once again.

Yasmeena prayed that he was right, that the world was coming to save the imprisoned and dying of Kuwait. Given the current prison turmoil, she believed that her prayers had been answered.

Yasmeena peered from behind her treasured curtains, watching as the armed guards ran past. She heard the jingling of cell keys and the clanking of cell doors. She glanced at the clock still perched atop the small table in the hallway. The time was five o'clock in the afternoon, the time most in the prison circus ate a meal, but no one was eating now.

Two of the older guards passed her cell. Each carried a large pistol in one hand and with the other pulled their women by their long hair. Both girls being dragged were young Kuwaitis recently apprehended. The poor girls were straining to dig their bare heels into the concrete flooring, trying to prevent the unavoidable. Their rapists were pulling them outside the prison. Both had obviously been forewarned that they were to be executed. Both were pleading to live. Although Yasmeena felt horrible for their plight, she was relieved that Lana was not to be seen. Her throat tightened as she considered what this day might bring to the sweetest girl she had ever known.

When one of the guards glanced to see Yasmeena witness the activity, he flashed a filthy look in her direction. Yasmeena shivered in fear, the curtain slipping from her fingers before she slunk out of view. Fearful that the mean-eyed man would take it upon himself to execute her, too, she concealed herself as best she could behind the plastic curtain that obscured her toilet area.

For the first time since being kidnapped and imprisoned, Yasmeena longed to see the Captain. Her heart told her that while his men might execute her along with all the other girls in the prison, he would not.

Yasmeena recognized that the Captain's former life of mediocrity no longer appealed to him. New hopes and dreams were intertwined with becoming a husband to four women. Yasmeena knew too that she was the heart and the face of that dream. The Captain had boasted that he would escort the desirable Yasmeena back to his village to display her beauty. She knew that he felt a strong urge to brag that such a woman could not get enough of him. With a beautiful young wife and pilfered cash from Kuwait, the dreary military man would finally come into the prominence he felt was his due. He would be an

144

important sheik in his village, a man of influence and promise. That's when he would walk alongside the big men of Iraq, and all who had scorned him previously would now look at him with eyes teeming with respect and envy.

Kuwait had given him his chance. Never again would he be given the opportunity to be a contender for the splendid life of a wealthy sheik. He *could not*, he *would not*, allow the dream to slip away.

Yasmeena was roused from her deep thoughts when she heard the dreaded familiar clang. The door to her cell was flung open with a clear urgency. She held her breath in fear until she heard the Captain speak her name. Her limbs were so weak she could barely move. Instead she hobbled like an ancient Chinese lady who had spent her life lounging on a silk-covered chair because her feet had been bound so tight that her little stubs had grown no larger than a flower blossom. She shuffled and tottered as she made her way to her Captain.

He obviously found endearing her expression of fear and total dependence. Even in the midst of this crisis, he found a smile.

"Why are you hiding, Yasmeena?"

"I am afraid," she admitted in a voice so soft he could barely hear her. "Your men have gone crazy. For the past hour they have been running in circles." She trembled. "Some have executed their women. What is happening?"

He took her small hands in his large ones and pulled her down. "Sit."

She sat, grateful to slump to her mat.

"It is as I thought. I have a good source telling me that Baghdad will soon issue orders for us to leave Kuwait."

Her throat was so dry her response was a hoarse croak. "Oh?"

He wasted no time. "I am waiting for the order. When it comes, we will have to leave." He paused, releasing his grip to caress her with his hands, a man obsessed with her body no matter the urgency of the current circumstances. "I cannot take you with me."

His words made her as happy as a child being told that all the presents ever dreamed of would soon magically appear. Yasmeena struggled to hold back laughter. That was before she remembered his warning that no witnesses would be left to tell what had occurred in the prison circus. And so she lied, one more time, although her story felt clumsy and unbelievable. "Oh please, you must take me with you. My Captain, you know that I cannot live without you."

He smiled pleasingly, accepting her words as true, his actions almost human for the first time since she met him, a man in love and affected by his woman's feelings. "I know how you love me. I know you cannot live without me. So I have a plan."

He released her hands and reached into his pants pocket. "Here, you take this," and he pushed a wad of U.S. dollars bound by a rubber band into her hands, "And this." He held out a crumpled piece of paper with writing on both sides. "Here is my information. It is my full name and the name of my good friend Abdullah in Basra. Here are directions to find his home in Basra. As soon as all of this is over, make your way out of Kuwait, come to Basra and contact my friend. You can trust him. He will find me. We will get married in Basra and then I will take you home to introduce you to my family."

Like a tsunami that washes away all that was before, worry faded as relief flowed through Yasmeena's entire being, from the brain in her head to her shaky limbs.

She was going to live!
She was going to live!
She was going to live!

She arranged her face as best she could, trying to present herself as a woman helplessly in love. "I will come. At the first minute, I will come to you."

He leaned in and kissed her. He whispered, "You are my woman. You will be my favorite wife." He grinned. "We will do it every day, like a honeymoon. We will never stop. Come to me, the minute this is over."

"Yes. Yes. I will come."

Overwhelmed by lust for her beauty, the Captain started to remove his belt. "Take off your clothes," he ordered. "We must do it one more time before I take you away."

Yasmeena froze, her mind had already settled nicely into a perfect future when she would never again have to submit her body to this man. "Are you sure? Do we have time?" she stammered.

"*Captain!*" An agitated voice of one of the Iraqi soldiers came from the prison office. "*Captain?*"

Yasmeena's Captain looked at her in regret and sorrow. "You are right. There is no time. Get a few things. You need to go."

Yasmeena grabbed her bag, tossing in the dollars and the note as to how to find the Captain in Basra. That's the moment she built her courage to ask, "What about Lana? What about the other women?"

"They are not your business, sweetie."

"Please," she pleaded desperately. "Let them go with me. Please."

From his brow to his chin, as though a mask was being poured over his face, the unyielding and ruthless face of her Captain slowly reappeared. Once again, nothing could touch his heart, which had hardened like stone. He was displeased and she knew it. "Shut up. We must get you to a safe place while there is time."

Frantic to save her Kuwaiti friend, Yasmeena took a big risk that she knew might incur her Captain's wrath. "Lana? At least Lana? Please, I beg you."

147

The Captain was unmoved by Yasmeena's anxiety for her friend.

"She is not your problem. Do not ask me again. You must go. Now."

Tears came to Yasmeena's eyes, but the Captain never noticed. He grabbed her firmly by her upper arm. "Let us go."

Yasmeena was blinded by those sudden tears. She knew that if Lana's fate was left to the beast the young girl would be tortured until the last moment of possible captivity before being murdered. But Yasmeena had no choice. She stumbled alongside her Captain.

In the hallway they passed several of the prison rapists, men now tense with nervousness. One of the older guards stepped in front of them. "I will do that for you, my Captain."

That's when Yasmeena realized that the men believed she was being taken to be shot. Her heart fluttered in fear. Was it all a show? Had the Captain spoken false words about their future only to keep her calm? Was she to be shot? She whimpered and began to struggle and the Captain gripped her tighter. "Quiet!" he ordered.

"She is my concern," the Captain answered abruptly. "Go back to your own problems. I will return shortly. Empty the prison now," he said in a knowing voice that Yasmeena believed meant that the women were to be killed.

The men said nothing more, although when Yasmeena stole a quick look at their faces, she thought they looked rather pleased to see what they assumed to be the end of the small Lebanese woman who had won their Captain's heart.

Events moved quickly from that moment. Her Captain drew his handgun, spurring her fears to mount. As if cued that violence was about to overtake the entire prison, the rapists scattered, running throughout the

148

prison and opening cell doors. The unseen women's voices began to weep and plead for their lives.

Yasmeena listened but did not hear Lana's voice, nor did she see the beast. She fervently hoped that one of the American bombs had fallen on his head and that he had disappeared from this earth in a puff of black smoke. If he was dead, perhaps Lana would live.

Once outside, the Captain yanked Yasmeena toward the back of the building.

In a rush, all her breath left her body. His reassuring words were lies. *She was going to be shot!*

But then the Captain looked quickly back to see if any of his men had followed. He switched directions, moving faster than her feet could follow as he ran toward a military vehicle, half dragging, half pushing her until she was unceremoniously dumped inside. "Get down," he hissed.

Darkness was coming soon, but Yasmeena knew that freedom was near. Perhaps sunrise would bring liberty to the beleaguered city. She wanted to see what was happening but the Captain cupped her head with his hand. "Stay down, I said!"

The Captain started the engine, but before driving away, he discharged several rounds of ammunition from his open window. Yasmeena clasped her hands to her mouth to keep from screaming in fear. What was he doing? Did he feel the need to trick his men, to make them believe that he had executed her?

He left the prison behind, the wheels of the vehicle spinning. Once the prison was out of sight, he hurriedly told her, "Okay. Listen to me. I am taking you to a mosque. Go inside and find a place to hide. Get inside a storeroom or closet and stay there. Kuwait City is going to go crazy. I doubt anyone will leave their homes to go to pray. Stay there until you can hear nothing of an army. Stay until it feels safe. Then make your way to the home of your friend."

Yasmeena said nothing. She was too frightened to speak. Perhaps it was all a lie.

But the Captain meant what he had said. She would live. He stopped at a small neighborhood mosque. "Get out. Go inside. The city will soon be filled with danger. Yasmeena, do *not* come out until you hear silence."

She gripped the handle of her bag and jumped from the vehicle, looking back at the man who was her torturer and rapist. She kept herself from saying all the words she had dreamed of saying, that he was nothing more than a murderer and a rapist and that she despised him. Surprisingly, in the midst of loathing, she experienced a spark of affection that he had saved her from a dusty grave. She bobbed her head up and down, so emotional she found it difficult to speak, but the lies continued, even to the end. "I will see you in Basra," she promised in a shaky voice.

He nodded grimly, "Yes. In Basra, you will be mine again." He moved the vehicle slowly away from her, waving his hand in farewell, promising her, "Until Basra!"

And with his heartfelt pledge of living to fuck her yet again another day, another place, another time, her rapist sped away into the night shouting loudly, "Until Basra! Until Basra!"

Chapter Fifteen: The Mini Captain

The instant the military vehicle was out of sight, Yasmeena hoisted the small bag to her back, then lifted off like an airplane. Her torso became a powerful engine with arms that became wings and legs that moved like fast-spinning wheels. She was racing through the Kuwaiti neighborhood like an Olympian. Suddenly every bodily pain was forgotten and she was capable of enormous physical feats. She was a young woman running from certain death and back into the promise of life. Her newfound strength was such that she was convinced she could run straight through the country of Kuwait and into the desert! Perhaps she would become a nomad, living on the ground, under the sky, and loving life. But then again she just might dash across the desert and run across the border into friendly Saudi Arabia, or perhaps dash to the seashore and dive into the Arabian Sea and swim without pausing through twenty kilometers of rough currents to drag her body up on the Failaka Island, remaining there until all danger passed.

Her mind matched her keen body strength, suddenly a thing of impenetrable steel. Her thoughts were as focused as the most brilliant thinker. She bared her teeth in a smile, sensing the rush of cool air across her lips and teeth and into her mouth, which she opened wide in a sense of joy. She had outwitted her Captain yet again. The man knew nothing of her if he thought she would blindly follow his commands. Never would she consider obeying his insipid order to hide in a mosque familiar to him so that he might have the chance to change his mind and return to reclaim her body as his own.

Yasmeena had finally regained her freedom and she was going to remain free.

Yasmeena was in a neighborhood unknown to her, but she kept running, oblivious of startled looks from those witnessing a small woman in a brightly colored dress running past Kuwaiti citizens scurrying about the city. Obviously rumors had spread that the winds of power had shifted. The dictator in Baghdad had been shown the light. The world would not continue to tolerate his neighborly grasp of Kuwait and he must vacate the little country if he was going to keep his bloody hold on his own country of Iraq.

Yasmeena quite possibly would have run forever. Her pace was so fast that when she rounded a corner she accidentally collided into a family of Kuwaitis spilling out of their automobile. She smashed into a young Kuwaiti teenage boy about her own size. Both were so startled by the collision that neither uttered a sound as they rolled around like spirited kittens. But the boy's mother squawked like one of those enormous feathered forest birds, shocking Yasmeena back into the moment. Once again she experienced ordinary human thoughts and pains. Wheezing like an aging pneumonia patient, she tried to push herself off the ground, but could not.

When the family finally understood that the feared attacker of their son was just a small woman who was clearly running away from danger, the father gently lifted Yasmeena by her arms and raised her to her feet. He quickly asked, "What's wrong? Are you being chased by soldiers?"

Yasmeena looked into the kindly faces of that family, a father, a mother, four daughters and two sons, and knew that she could never reveal the reality of her rape, torture and imprisonment. This was clearly a virtuous family who would not know how to process such reprehensible deeds such as kidnapping and torture and rape. Besides, Yasmeena would be humiliated. These moral people would not want to hear about the brutality she experienced, the beastly acts she had endured and at times encouraged, just so that she might survive.

Yes, this was an entire family of Lana's ilk. All would fight to the death before submitting to the revolting cruelties Yasmeena had withstood. And so she effortlessly voiced an insignificant lie, wondering as she spoke if she might ever regain the purity of her previous existence. Since childhood, she had always prided herself on being a girl who never stooped to deceit, but after many weeks of lying daily to her rapist, she feared she had become immune to the malady of lying. "Yes," she said, "some soldiers started chasing me and caught me and put me in their vehicle. I ran away when they stopped to arrest the driver of a vehicle that did not have an Iraqi tag." Yasmeena knew that brave Kuwaitis would always defy Baghdad's explicit command to replace Kuwaiti automobile tags with Iraqi tags, even if it meant they would be arrested and sometimes executed. The Baghdad butcher meant business, even when it came to such mundane matters as automobile tags.

The family was sympathetic, but they were in a rush too. The conqueror and conquered alike had caught the excitement of the day and danger filled the Kuwaiti air. The father and mother urged their children and Yasmeena to rush into the safety of their home.

Once inside the family home Yasmeena was settled into the most comfortable chair. The mother draped a pricey diaphanous coverlet over Yasmeena's lap and legs. One of the daughters served some refreshing cool yogurt. The women of the family surrounded her with kindness. They were too polite to press for answers and for that Yasmeena was tearfully grateful.

Yasmeena enjoyed a small amount of the food and drank a large glass of water. The mother escorted her into a bedroom suite, pointing out the bathroom and telling Yasmeena that she should refresh herself. She peered at Yasmeena and commented that she was small, the same size as their middle daughter, and that she would find some suitable clothing folded on the bed when she came out of her bath.

Soon the door was closed and Yasmeena was alone. She stood without moving, feeling herself still a participant in the nightmare she had lived for so many weeks. She allowed her thoughts to revisit the prison circus, to the hell where the other girls were still suffering, or possibly the place where their corpses were now sprawled. She winced at the thought of the violence that might have occurred there. Were lifeless eyes no longer watching for the evil men who had stolen the joy of youth and led them to an early grave? Just thinking of Lana's sweet nature and stoic acceptance of her fate, Yasmeena knew that she must risk the return and do what she could to bring Lana and the others to freedom, too. When, and how, she might do that, she did not know. If she could only go back to her Kuwaiti friend's home, she could surely convince those two brave sons to assemble a group of freedom fighters to charge the prison circus and release the young women held there.

But first she would gather her strength for the challenge ahead.

President Saddam Hussein
The Iraqi president announced on Baghdad radio that Iraqi troops were withdrawing from Kuwait and that the entire Iraqi Army would be out of the country by the end of the day.
—*Radio Baghdad*
February 26, 1991

Personal Testimony

"I asked my mother and my aunts and they were very adamant that troops left on February 26 around sunrise."
—Lujain, young Kuwaiti woman reporting to Jean Sasson

Personal Testimony

"February 25th 1991 was another day of occupation, and no one knew whether they [Iraqi army] were going to withdraw from Kuwait or not. The only thing we knew is that things were close to an end. Some Iraqis started withdrawing from Kuwait on February 25th around midnight, and then the rest of them started fleeing the country on February 26th around 1AM Kuwait time. We now celebrate the liberation of Kuwait on the 26th of every February."
—From Kuwaiti Abdul Rahman, friend of Kuwaiti Fares, friend of Jean Sasson

A few hours after the most soothing bath of her life, a thunderous noise woke Yasmeena from a deep sleep. A few moments passed before she remembered that she had eluded the Captain and was safe in the home of a kindly Kuwaiti family. The noise was so deafening she believed for a moment the Kuwaiti home that sheltered her was about to be struck by an airplane. She awaited her fate, scarcely believing her bad luck. Had she escaped her rapist and potential murderer only to be crushed and burned to death by a crashing airplane? The noise grew louder as she waited for death. But death did not come.

She looked at a clock and saw that the hour was extremely early, or extremely late. The time was one o'clock, whether morning or afternoon she could not be certain. She overheard her hosts shouting for their children to come quickly. Yasmeena grabbed the silky bathrobe left for her use and followed the strident voices of the parents as a guide. Running as fast as her extremely tender feet and sore thighs could take her she rushed to the second floor of the home where the family was gathered in a room used solely to watch television. A quick glance told Yasmeena that large double doors led out to a balcony.

After making certain that his entire family had assembled, the father gingerly opened the doors and slowly stepped out onto the dark balcony. That's when Yasmeena knew that it was in the early hours of the morning. The uproar they had heard grew even wilder through those open doors. An inquisitive Yasmeena joined the watchful father and his two sons even as the females in the family pleaded for Yasmeena to stay inside, to keep safe.

Yasmeena recoiled at the noisy spectacle on the streets underneath the balcony. Moments passed before she realized that the thunderous sound they heard was that of hundreds of roaring vehicles all across the city, their engines all being revved at once. The rumble of the machinery was so earsplittingly loud she felt pulled to rush inside. But Yasmeena refused to miss one millisecond of the disorderly departure of the shocked and alarmed Iraqi military. Thousands of armed men were rushing about trying to find a way to get out of Kuwait and back to Iraq. The happiest thought of all was her knowledge that her smug Captain and his haughty thugs were at that moment in the crowd of panicky soldiers, experiencing fear similar to the fright they had so arrogantly imposed on Kuwaiti civilians, and for that she was more exultant than she had been in a long time. They had ruled like thuggish kings, and now they were paying their dues for the macabre liberties they had taken with an entire nation, and yes, against young innocent women.

She stood staring, mouth open wide and hands covering her ears. All of Kuwait City was in pandemonium. After nearly seven months of occupation, the Iraqi army was really leaving.

The evacuation process seemed interminable. Like a cancer being forcibly removed from its unwilling host, Iraqi soldiers continued to spill from occupied buildings and villas to leap into any and all modes of transportation. The roads swarmed with military vehicles, civilian cars and trucks, all crammed with soldiers.

Yasmeena heard the expected but distinctive rumble of army tanks. Fleeing tanks were pushing forward on the city streets as fast as they could travel, their Iraqi drivers unmindful of the clotted traffic ahead: hundreds of military vehicles filled with their own comrades. Over the roar of engines came the fainter sound of dying men screaming in agony as the tanks rolled over and crushed the stalled vehicles as easily as if they were toys.

Yasmeena looked on in disbelief. The Iraqi army was maiming and killing its own. After a brief time of reflection, Yasmeena decided this was a suitable conclusion to the occupation. She felt the hate of a woman who had been brutally raped for months. She felt the disdain of a woman who had witnessed the unspeakable brutalization of the youthful and innocent Lana. The rapists had taught her to hate, and she hated with a vengeance that would have been impossible for her before August 2, 1990.

Her host Kuwaiti father and sons turned from the balcony to sit with the women of the family and describe the unbelievable sights they had seen, but Yasmeena remained standing, alone and watchful, for several hours, waiting until the final vehicle with the last Iraqis departed the city. She knew that her Captain was in that mass of men, and that he was finally out of her life forever.

When the last rumbling vehicle vanished from sight, Yasmeena began planning her return to the prison circus. She gazed at the still-dark sky, but saw there was a

157

promise of sunrise. At first light, she would return to that place of horror, and search for Lana and the other women.

Morning could not come soon enough. Dressed neatly in the Kuwaiti daughter's pretty lilac-colored dress, her newly washed hair pulled back, Yasmeena stared through the automobile window at the groups of celebrating Kuwaitis as her host drove her to her Kuwaiti friend's home.

Upon their arrival, she learned from the family servants that the family was no longer in the country. About a week after Yasmeena disappeared from the roadblock, they grew fearful for the safety of their sons, since they had no idea if Yasmeena had been tortured into revealing their names. Therefore they had hired a skilled guide to escort them through the Kuwaiti and Saudi deserts into Saudi Arabia. But the family had left Yasmeena a note in the event she was still alive. The friendly note instructed her to feel free to remain in their home as if it were her own, and to make use of their automobiles or anything else she might need. They said they would return as soon as Kuwait was free.

Yasmeena did not know that as a volunteer helping the underground fighters she was a hero to those who knew of her sacrifice. Most believed that she had been executed for her attempted delivery of the flyers.

She was sad and happy all at once, for she had blessings and troubles all bound together in a neat package. She now had a place to stay, but no friends in the country who might help her. Despite her worries, she smiled as she said goodbye to the kindly father who had transported her. He promised to bring the family for a visit later, after the excitement in the city waned.

The moment he turned away from the villa, she immediately told the Sri Lankan male gardener and the

Filipina housemaid that she wanted them to go with her to the prison where she had been held. She had to know the condition of the other women who had been in prison with her.

War in the Gulf
Speaking on a satellite telephone with the Cable News Network, Col. Abu Fahad, a leader of Kuwaiti anti-Iraqi forces in Kuwait, said that when they retreated the Iraqis "took all these hostages, thousands of prisoners, with them as they left."
—*New York Times*
February 27, 1991

Kuwait City
Kuwaitis are celebrating the great victory! Car horns are blaring, many are displaying photographs of the Emir, and others are holding Kuwaiti flags. Men are dancing in the streets and women are crying from joy.
—Announcement from the Kuwaiti Embassy
Washington, D.C.
February 27, 1991

With her thoughts focused on the fate of the women she had left behind, Yasmeena did not join in the happy celebrations erupting throughout the city. Every neighborhood she passed through was filled with rejoicing Kuwaitis. They were as happy as a people could be. The day they had believed might never come was upon them. Men were dancing in the streets, and women were trilling and children were playing. Kuwaiti joy was boundless.

But the block surrounding the prison was eerily dark and silent. Had men from the neighborhood already explored the prison? Had the women already been freed? Or were they still locked in their cells? A fearless Yasmeena jumped from the car and ran inside, calling, "Lana? Lana?"

There was no reply.

Yasmeena passed her own empty cell without looking, rushing from one vacant cell to another. All the cell doors hung open, all cells emptied of their prisoners. With her heart in her throat, Yasmeena dashed into Lana's cell hoping for confirmation that her friend had survived, but she saw nothing to inspire confidence. Lana's sleeping mat and blanket were still there, as well as the ropes and chains that had been used to bind her. Yasmeena recoiled from the stench of infected wounds, blood and accumulated filth which still saturated the air of the cell.

Yasmeena spotted Lana's black gown spread out alongside Lana's dirty mat. Yasmeena plucked it from the floor and fingered the sheer gown, remembering the last time she had seen Lana's small body covered by the nightie. When she recognized numerous stains as dried pus and semen, she let it slip from her hand, shuddering at memories of the horrors Lana had endured while wearing the gown. She shivered, sorry that she had touched the gown, knowing that the beast had once stroked it with his own repugnant fingers.

At that moment Yasmeena remembered an awful truth. When the situation for the Iraqis began to unravel, the Captain had never bought her the writing material, nor had she questioned Lana further on the promised personal information. Due to nearly constant beatings and continued painful rapes, Lana had been in such a frail state for the past month that Yasmeena's time with the young girl had been spent discussing and treating injuries. Yasmeena's only goal had been to keep her friend alive.

How could Yasmeena ever find Lana's family now? She didn't even know Lana's family name. Lana remained fearful to confide that information to anyone, although she had planned to dictate all the information to Yasmeena.

Yasmeena reluctantly walked from the prison circus to the execution grounds, fearing that she might see there the bodies of all the women. But once again, there were no prisoners, wounded, dead or alive. She examined the dirt around the shooting post, and while dismayed to see splatters of blood mixed with dirt, felt a faint hope when she realized that the quantity of blood she was seeing was not enough to indicate the execution of fourteen women.

Where was the blood? Where were the women?

Had the Captain's men taken precious time to bury the women? Had they taken the women with them? Knowing Lana's beast rapist well, she recognized that he would have never allowed Lana her freedom. Was her wounded friend in one of those packed vehicles, making her way to Iraq to spend a life of misery with the beast?

A dispirited Yasmeena returned once more inside the prison circus to be certain that in her haste she had missed nothing. After rummaging through every cell but her own--and for what she did not know--Yasmeena finally left the prison circus for the last time.

The burden of Yasmeena's torment was yet to fully flower. That evening after eating a small bowl of yogurt, some stale bread and a sweet, she felt waves of nausea climbing from her belly to her throat. All the food she ate returned later as foul-tasting bile. Holding her hair away from her face as she leaned over the toilet, she had a creeping consciousness of looming ruin–she remembered that she had not seen her womanly blood for the past two months. In the midst of living her hellish ordeal, she had forgotten about it, in fact, perhaps vaguely aware that any

161

raped prisoner who was unable to hide a pregnancy from her rapist was quickly executed.

Yasmeena perched on the edge of the bed, eyes and mouth open wide, her hands clutched to her stomach she knew with a sureness she had never before known, that she was with child, pregnant by a man she loathed with her whole heart.

She whimpered like a wounded child, falling full body across the bed, her mind racing. Where would she go? Who could she turn to? Who could she trust to keep her dark secret?

She writhed in agony, her convulsive movements reminiscent of a pitiful fox she had once seen when her family was driving past one of the quaint hillside villages atop Mount Lebanon. Yasmeena and her sisters had cried out when they spied the fox sprawled by the winding roadside, its delicate paw clenched in the jaws of a small steel trap. The poor thing had dragged itself and the trap from the woods. Yasmeena had peered into its little face contorted in pain. She had pleaded with her father to stop the car, to do something. But her father would not risk being bitten by a fox. For a long time afterward Yasmeena could not erase the image from her mind: The poor fox trembling in pain. Knowing the Lebanese character as she did, she feared that no one would intervene. The poor animal most likely had died slowly and painfully.

She was now like the fox, in unrelenting agony and with no one help her.

Yasmeena's plan to bury the dreadful time of her imprisonment suddenly vanished. Before this final moment of bitter reality, she had so yearned to survive, hopeful for a second chance, desperate to resume a normal life so that she might leave behind the wretched life of daily rapes. She had plotted her reentry into ordinary life, prepared to divulge only that she had been arrested and imprisoned for being a part of the Kuwaiti underground. She had no plans to ever admit being raped. As far as marriage, she never wanted another man to touch her body. She would refuse any offers of marriage and would live her life as a single woman, over time becoming a favored spinster auntie to her nieces and nephews.

Now how could she disguise the fact she had been raped when the Captain's baby was nestled inside her? She sat numb and mute, like a pale marble statue she had once seen in one of those enormous museums in France. Slowly a new strategy drew together like a weapon in her mind, affording her new resolve and strength.

Yasmeena cried out, "I will never bear the child of a monster!"

Epilogue: The Baby Villa

Yasmeena was pacing in her bedroom. Everything had gone wrong. After discovering she was pregnant, she had prayed to God for a miscarriage, for a natural and divine cleansing of her body, knowing that she could never care for, or love, a baby of rape, a baby of a monster. But God did not answer her prayer. Other than the stomach sickness, she remained healthy with her blossoming belly growing larger by the day.

Mentally she found herself picturing the baby's face. She knew in her heart that the baby was a boy, a tiny replica of the monster who had planted him there. She imagined the baby's little flabby body, a mini reproduction of the Captain's saggy figure. She felt her fingers advancing toward her private opening, and those fingers suddenly had a life of their own and they were going to rip the tiny Captain out of her body and flush it down the toilet. Once her fingers tentatively probed her vagina, but her body opening was so small that she now wondered in amazement how it was that the Captain got his big thing inside her.

But now she had a more pressing question. How would the Captain's baby get out of such a small opening? Like most Arab girls, she was naïve about men and women and sexual matters and had never given much thought to the medical details of reproduction.

Her memories combined with her current reality to create a fear that paralyzed her. Her fright was so profound that she could only weep and pace. How could she solve this baby problem when the baby was growing bigger by the day?

Waiting for a miracle, she did nothing. The baby remained inside her until it was too late. One day while walking past a mirror, she unintentionally caught a view of her body profile. Yasmeena gulped, realizing for the first time that there was a decided bulge on her once-flat belly. How did the baby get that big so quickly? Then she reminded herself that the bump was in fact the Captain! He was a big man. His seed would produce big babies. She lightly thumped her belly and then lost all rational thought. She screeched, *"Get out! Get out!"* She sobbed, pleading, "Please get out. Get out. Please get out."

But the baby stayed, nestled happily inside her body.

Although she longed to telephone her mother to tell her family that she was still alive, she could not. First, the Iraqis had destroyed the telephone service and it would take time for the Kuwaiti government to make repairs. Second, she could not confess her pregnancy to her family. If she confessed the pregnancy, she had to confess the rapes and all that led up to her arrest and imprisonment. She could not do that to her parents. She could not darken the old age of her parents by revealing such a sordid tale. The decision was made: She could not talk to her parents until the baby was gone, one way or another.

Yasmeena's personal crisis kept building. As soon as the Kuwaiti telephone lines were repaired, she received an international call from her Kuwaiti hosts. They told her something of their own trauma, the shock of her disappearance, the fear that Iraqis would soon kick in their door and arrest them all. They could not stand the suspense of not knowing, so they slipped from the city and drove across the desert, luckily failing to run into any Iraqis. From Saudi Arabia they flew to London where they remained in their apartment in that city.

They were all alive, thanks be to God. Considering that the two sons had been active members in the Kuwaiti underground, they were luckier than most. Many courageous youths, males and females, had been arrested, tortured and executed.

Now Yasmeena's friend was ecstatic that Yasmeena had also survived and was waiting for them at their home. She wanted to know everything, she said, but considering the international call, would wait until the family returned to Kuwait to hear Yasmeena's full tale. Like all Kuwaitis who had survived the early months of the occupation before fleeing, they could not quite believe their good luck that their country had been returned to them intact, although they had been told that much of the infrastructure was destroyed.

She babbled for what seemed like hours to Yasmeena, whose side of the conversation consisted of little more than grunts and sighs. Her friend finally ended the call, but not before promising that the family would return as soon as the utilities were functioning and all was safe, for they had heard that Kuwait still held danger and that some celebrating Kuwaitis had been wounded or killed by discarded landmines and unexploded bombs.

After that call, the bed became Yasmeena's sanctuary. Her prolonged melancholy lasted three full days. Knowing she had to do *something* about the unwanted fetus, she made the biggest mistake of her life by going to a government hospital and unburdening her sorrows to a nurse, asking for advice on what she might do. She foolishly believed that the nurse might recommend a safe method of getting rid of the baby. Careful not to tell the entire saga of the previous few months, she revealed only that she had been raped by an enemy soldier and was now left with an unwanted baby budding inside her.

To Yasmeena's horrified disbelief, the nurse failed to keep her confidence and instead slipped out of the examining room to call in a male doctor who was told everything confidential Yasmeena had confessed. The serious-faced doctor reacted in the same manner as many in her culture might behave. He glared at her in stern disapproval as though she was foolishly responsible for being abducted and raped. "Why did you agree to transport resistance materials?" he inquired. Yes, she was the reason for the baby problem, rather than the rapist. He cleared his throat and pulled on his untidy beard and finally blurted out that he was unable to make any decisions, that the government was undertaking to solve the problem, trying to decide what was best for all concerned. Meanwhile, the government was confining all single women impregnated by the enemy soldiers. She would wait out her pregnancy in a government-managed villa, and she would receive free medical care. That's the first time Yasmeena heard that all pregnant rape victims would be cared for by the Kuwaiti government. The news was good, and bad, all at the same time. While it was acceptable to have someone to help care for her, she was nervous about losing control of her own destiny.

After that sobering conversation, Yasmeena was rudely escorted from the hospital as though she was a tainted lawbreaker into a rickety van with torn leather seats and filthy carpets. The van transported her to a wealthy section of the city, stopping in front of a large pink-hued villa.

Yasmeena was told to go inside where she was met by two middle-aged nurses from India. After stating her name and age and estimated time of being impregnated, she was guided to a small room where she was invited to make herself at home, to have a shower and go to bed, get some rest. She would be served three meals a day and could take those meals in her room, or in the general dining hall.

At that same time she was told that she was one of thirty victims living in the villa. As was the case in the prison circus, she was soon to discover that there was a variety of nationalities in the baby villa, the nickname the attending staff had given to the villa of confinement.

Yasmeena's life in the baby villa passed in silence and in a blur. Choosing isolation, she ate in her room, accepting quietly the food the staff set before her. Everything was tasteless, anyhow. She calmly swallowed the vitamins the nurses dispensed. She lay silently while the doctors examined her. She listened quietly to the nurses who whispered that the Kuwaiti government was soon going to call a meeting of parliament to decide whether or not the girls would be allowed late-term abortions, something every girl and woman in the baby villa said that they wanted.

When told that the baby inside her was approximately four months old, she realized that she had been pregnant for longer than she realized, almost from the beginning of her capture. Strangely, she had never noticed any symptoms but attributed her heedlessness to the shock of all that had happened to her.

But now all she could think about was the Kuwaiti parliament and when they would meet to decide on the fates of so many pregnant girls and women. She prayed to her God for the right to have a late-term abortion. She didn't care how old the baby was. She only wanted the baby to vanish. How nice it would be if the baby could disappear in a puff of smoke, to be out of her life forever. Just like the Captain: Gone, gone, gone forever. When she thought that the Captain might have believed her promises, and that he might be impatiently waiting for her in Basra so that he might rape her again, she trembled in revulsion. She hoped he was dead. She hoped that his corpse was rotting in the hot desert sun and his flesh was being eaten by scavengers.

When excited nurses offered news about the massacre on the road to Basra, telling the story as a sort of consolation prize to the women who had been so abused, Yasmeena listened in silence. Her emotions were mixed. She had an image of all those threatening penises being charred off the bodies of the rapists, and that was a pleasurable vision. Those men should never again know the joy of raping a woman. She wished that the Captain, the monster rapist and all the rapists in the prison circus had suffered dreadfully as they burned to death when those huge bombs fell on the departing convoy.

But she was terrified that Lana and other innocent Kuwaitis had gotten caught in the conflagration. Everyone knew that several thousand innocent Kuwaitis and various other nationalities had been taken by the Iraqis on that hurried exodus out of Kuwait. What was the fate of those innocent people?

In the quiet hours of the baby villa, Yasmeena felt Lana's absence every minute, every hour, every day. If only Lana were with her in this villa, Yasmeena could better accept her fate. If only Lana had survived the monster rapist, there would be cause for joy.

During the first week Yasmeena forced herself to meet every pregnant girl housed in the villa. Although sorry for the girls whom she knew had endured a nightmarish ordeal similar to her own, she didn't remember them or their stories for a moment longer than it took her to close the doors to their bedrooms and walk away. Yasmeena was looking only for one face. She had never given up hope that her dear friend Lana had survived.

But Lana was nowhere to be found.

Yasmeena met no one in whom she could confide. Her anger and fear bubbled inside her, producing a toxic brew that was eating her insides like that slow-acting acid the Iraqi soldiers had bragged about. She had been a peaceful girl for her entire life, loathing war and violence,

169

but now she was alone for too many hours on her small hard bed. In her solitude she stewed about Lana, fretted about her own fate, and simmered with anger and fear over a baby who meant nothing to her, nothing more than a diminutive version of the Captain, the man who had raped and tortured her for many long months. The Captain was still inside her in the form of his baby, like a parasite attached to her innards.

She hated the Captain and she hated his baby.

During Yasmeena's fifth week in the baby villa one of the kindest of the nurses came to reveal an exciting secret. The government had invited a writer, a female from the United States, to come to the villa to meet with the women and to hear their stories. The writer would then write about the rapes and the murder and the horror of it all and tell their stories to the world. The girls did not have cause for concern because the writer had lived for many years in the Middle East and understood their Arab culture and the cultural shame involved with sexual assault. She would not reveal their true names and would even change some identifying particulars of their lives so as to build a veil of protection around the girls.

But a book was important because it was the only way the world would discover the horrific crimes that had been committed upon their bodies. The nurse confessed to Yasmeena that she believed that the government was correct and that all the crimes committed against Kuwaitis should be publicized to all. They had been told by the Kuwaiti government that the girls should be encouraged to trust and to talk to this female writer.

Yasmeena said little but thought a lot. After the nurse left, she considered all aspects of the situation, finally concluding that if the writer did not tell her true name, and changed some identifying details about her, she yearned to talk, she wanted everyone to know exactly what Arab men had done to Arab women.

Yasmeena was burning inside and decided that she would be the first to volunteer to meet with the American writer.

The American writer came the following day to find Yasmeena impatiently waiting. For the past twenty-four hours she had thought only about this interview. Perhaps by telling Lana's story, and her own, maybe all those who did not survive would be remembered by the whole world. The book could be a special tribute to the memory of every girl and woman who was raped.

Yasmeena decided that no matter how difficult it might be to verbally relive the ghastly memories, she would tell everything, all the gory details of her imprisonment and rape and of the ghastly acts committed upon Lana and the other women. The entire Arab world should--and would--know what Arab men had done to Arab women.

The American writer was very pleasant, warm in her greetings and had a kindly manner. Yasmeena realized that the woman felt sympathy for her situation and this feeling helped diminish her misgivings. She was at ease.

Her only concern was that a Kuwaiti man accompanied the woman. After she learned that the man had remained inside Kuwait and had fought against the occupiers, she felt somewhat better. Despite this, she was not comfortable for the man to hear the most graphic details of her sexual abuse. Thankfully the Kuwaiti was a sensitive man and seemed to realize the privacy needed without her having to say a word in protest. He casually mentioned that since she spoke good English and would not need a translator, he would wait in another area when she was ready to speak openly.

171

And so Yasmeena sat at a small table facing the woman. She had thought the confession of those raping days would be difficult to reveal, but it was not. This was the first time she had been able to voice her misery and her anger. When she began to talk, she could not stop. She talked slowly but frankly, not wanting to leave anything out. She affirmed all that had happened to her and what she knew had happened to Lana from the first day of the occupation to the last. She had been in the country for every minute since August 2, 1990, so she had lots to tell.

The American writer was visibly affected but she did not interrupt to ask questions. She occasionally wrote a few sentences on the pages of a notebook and several times Yasmeena asked to see the notes to make sure there was nothing which would lead readers directly to Yasmeena. But mainly the writer sat and stared into Yasmeena's eyes and on occasion stroked Yasmeena's hands and sometimes uttered her concern, saying, "I am sorry. I am so sorry."

Yasmeena had no way to keep time, no way of knowing that she talked nonstop from early in the morning until late at night with only a few pauses to sip from her glass of apple juice. When she finally stopped talking, she saw that the American writer was listening with a sad expression on her face. She was fighting to hold back tears.

When the American writer composed herself, she told Yasmeena that she was worried about her and wondered when she would be calling her family.

Yasmeena burst into tears for the first time and replied, "I will never call them. I am dead to them. I cannot destroy their happiness by telling them my story. I do not deserve them. I did something very dishonorable to pretend to love my rapist. My family would never forgive me."

The American writer quietly disagreed and insisted that Yasmeena had not only been brave, but she had been clever. Her actions brought her out of the ordeal alive and that would be what was most important to her family. Yasmeena could not have stopped the rapes no matter what she did. But she was able to foil her execution. The author was convinced that the Captain would have killed her had Yasmeena not been a talented actress. She deserved accolades for her acting abilities. Had she not convinced the Captain that she was in love with him, she, too, would have been executed, just like so many other girls and women.

The greatest victory was to have lived. Now she was giving crucial testimony so that all the women would receive some justice just by the world knowing of their suffering. What would it have accomplished for Yasmeena to have forfeited her life? Nothing: just another innocent girl shot. One day the story would be told and perhaps someone influential in the world would work to classify such rapes an atrocity of great enormity and that the punishment would finally fit the crime. Perhaps by living, she had helped many other women in the world. Yasmeena was a hero in the author's mind.

Yasmeena could only croak, "No. No." For too long she had thought of herself as dishonorable. In her mind, the word "hero" could never apply to a Lebanese girl named Yasmeena.

The American writer pressed further, volunteering to meet with Yasmeena's family. The writer had been to Lebanon several times and had intimate Lebanese friends. Perhaps she could speak to Yasmeena's family and guide them to be at ease with Yasmeena's decision to do what she had to do to save her life.

"No. No. I cannot face them. I cannot." Yasmeena, who was always a clever girl, changed the unpleasant topic and said, "Talk to the other women, too. Then think about what Arab men did to Arab women. *Make this the theme of your writings: What Arab men did to their women! Shame on them! Shame on them! Shame on them!*"

The American writer leaned forward and embraced Yasmeena in a heartfelt hug, and Yasmeena gave her an affectionate gaze.

But the embrace broke through Yasmeena's resolve not to tell what was really on her mind. Without thinking she leaped to her feet and startled herself and the writer by verbalizing a great secret that had weighed on her mind for the past month. She began to weep, but through her tears she stared directly at the American writer and roared, "I don't want to be an Arab! I don't want to be an Arab! Look what the Arabs do to one another. I want to be a Jew. I want to be an Israeli Jew. I want to go and live in Israel. The Jews would not do this to *their* women. They would not. But the Arabs do it to *their* women! What does that say about us? I am an Arab! I once was a proud Arab. But now I hate being an Arab. And you know what? I will no longer be an Arab. I will be a Jew if they will have me. Will you help me? Will you help me? Talk to someone! Ask them if I can come to Israel and be a Jew! That is what I want. I never want to be where Arab men can attack me, never again!" Yasmeena burst into heartrending sobs for the first time in a long time.

"Shush, Shush. You must take care, Yasmeena. Tell no one else what you have just told me." The American writer was quickly anxious that others in the villa would hear her shouting out her desire to be a Jew, to be an Israeli, the most hated people in the world for most Arabs. But Yasmeena could not be quieted and as the American writer whispered kind words to her, she shrieked as loud as Lana, *"I don't want to be an Arab! Arab men rape and murder their women! I don't want to be an Arab! I want to be a Jew!"*

And then Yasmeena lost control of her emotions completely and fell across the table, sobbing so loudly that concerned medical staff ran to peek into the room. The American writer reassured the staff, saying, "She is okay.

She is upset from reliving the memories. It is okay. Do not worry."

Through the fog of her grief, Yasmeena acknowledged that, "I know you are protecting me. I, too, know that my own people will turn against me. But I know in my heart that if any woman had suffered with me, she would agree with what I am saying. How can Arab men systemically rape Arab women? How can they?"

After another hour of weeping and talking, the American writer said that she must leave, but she pleaded with Yasmeena to reconsider contacting her family in Lebanon, for the writer believed that Yasmeena could only heal in the arms of those who most loved her.

But Yasmeena had decided and nothing would change her future plans. She hugged the American writer, thanked her, and said that she hoped that the story of the prison circus and the innocent women confined within, would one day be published and placed in bookstores. "I will be looking for the book in Israel," she said with a determined tight smile.

As Yasmeena walked away to return to her solitary confinement and to wait for the birth of what she believed with her whole heart was a monster child, she loosed one loud sob, then spoke forcefully enough for the writer to overhear, "I *will* become a Jew. *I will!*"

A Note from the Author

After arriving in Kuwait to personally view the damage done to the country and meet with the people who had remained during the long months of occupation, the Kuwaiti Crown Prince and the Minister of Information, generously offered me a few stories that they claimed to intentionally keep from other writers or journalists. I believe it was their way of thanking me for writing *The Rape of Kuwait*, the only book written about the individual suffering of the Kuwaitis who experienced the invasion.

And so after several weeks in the country, I was given the opportunity to meet with raped and pregnant girls and women. I was told that I was free to tell their stories, although I was asked not to take photographs or to identify the victims by name. However, I was told that I was free to describe in full the horror the women endured as sex slaves.

Although I was already feeling overwhelmed by the incessant stories of Kuwaiti loss and anguish, when I entered the pink villa housing pregnant girls and women, I was presented with a scene unmatched in all the country for grief and misery.

While there were a number of serious-faced nurses from Sri Lanka and India, women who were lovingly caring for the raped victims, I was also presented with scores of desolate girls and women, their big bellies an obvious source of unmistakable heartache and anguish, rather than joyful expectation so common to pregnant women. Gazing at the misery on those young faces warned me that that the depth of my own horror had not yet been reached.

Although the women were housed in a luxurious villa supplied by the Kuwaiti government, and all were receiving free medical care, their sorrowful faces reminded me of photographs I had seen of survivors of liberated World War II concentration camps. Over the course of three days I would speak with a number of exceedingly depressed and anxious women, but it was the agony of one specific woman, a woman by the name of Yasmeena, who focused my heart and soul on the most tragic story I have ever heard.

After a very long and exhausting day of emotional and ragged testimony of personal anguish and suffering, I finally pulled away from Yasmeena, walking slowly down the corridor and pushing through the heavy door. As I left Yasmeena, my heart whispered to me, "You will remember this woman and her words forever."

And, I have.

I left the baby villa and joined Soud in his automobile so that he could drive me back to the hotel. Once alone in my room, I sat and read over my notes and added other comments. While re-reading the words I wrote, I was reminded that in a world of brave women, Yasmeena was one of the most courageous women I had ever met. I knew that her choice to live took enormous courage, for what could be more difficult than to endure brutal rapes with a cooperative smile.

While it was not necessary to make a single note, for I knew that Yasmeena's oral history would forever remain etched in my mind and in my heart, even without a single reminder, I wanted and needed to remain busy.

Even late in the evening, and feeling the creep of exhaustion, I could not sleep. Instead, I paced, and while walking back and forth from the door to the bed to the sitting area, I suffered a range of emotions. Yes, I was relieved that the war was over. Yes, I was happy that the prisons were empty. But in my mind, I knew that the girls and women I had just met were prisoners still, and that in their minds, they would always be prisoners. They could take some small comfort from the fact they had survived a hell like no other. The life that lay ahead could only be better. One can go to hell only once. And for the girls and the women of the prison circus, that's a trip already taken.

Further details about Yasmeena & Lana

Yasmeena is a real person and her story is true. Lana is a real person and her story is true. I'm sorry that I never met Lana, for that would mean that the young woman had survived, but sadly, I only know of her through Yasmeena's memories of the days when she and Lana shared their hellish fates.

Yasmeena failed to locate Lana.

I have often speculated on Lana's fate. Perhaps Lana was one of the many Kuwaitis taken with the Iraqi soldiers back into Iraq. Perhaps Lana was one of the thousands of Iraqis and their Kuwaiti hostages trapped in the long convoys on the inland highway to Basra--the miles and miles of burned--out vehicles along the "Highway of Death."

I visited the "Highway of Death" with Soud A. Al-Mutawa, the kindly Kuwaiti banker who was my voluntary driver and translator. Soud and I were silent as we gazed at the carnage. Although we were both glad that Kuwait was free, we found no joy in that road of death.

It is entirely possible that Lana was one of the scorched skeletons in those vehicles. Or perhaps Lana was executed by her beastly rapist before he fled Kuwait. That was her likely outcome, although we will probably never know the fate of Lana.

As far as the rapists, I've often asked myself: Were they ever punished for their crimes? Perhaps, yes. Perhaps, no. If they made their way safely back to their cities or villages in Iraq, then they were never punished. But perhaps they died beneath the Allied bombs. Perhaps their remains lay in some of the destroyed vehicles on the infamous "Highway of Death."

We will never know their fate unless they recognize themselves in the pages of this book and admit to their crimes. This is something I do not expect to happen, though I would be pleased if such confessions were made. I would like to ask Yasmeena's Captain, a man born to a woman, married to a woman, and the father of daughters, one question: How could you abuse innocent women?

I met Yasmeena in Kuwait after the war, exactly as described in this book. She was the only rape victim who was sincerely eager to share the most intimate details of what it is like to be brutally raped, day after day, night after night. Other victims were more guarded, reluctant to reveal the most private aspects of being sexually attacked, although they were willing to acknowledge that they had been held and raped repeatedly.

And so I sat and listened, hearing the graphic details pour from Yasmeena. She spared no particulars, describing the men who were their jailors, the women who were held, the details of the sexual acts so violently committed upon the women.

I heard everything, and I was humbled by the strength of all the women, but I was most moved by the strength the very young Lana demonstrated in fighting her rapist with all her power. I was also inspired by Yasmeena's ability to outwit her rapist and to survive. She was strong and clever. She should be honored for saving her life, living to tell a story that no one would know were it not for her strength to survive.

I regret that I was unable to write this true story for a long time. At first, the story was so fresh, so new, so painful....and I feared that Yasmeena would be traced by someone working at the villa that housed the unfortunate women. What if her real name was given to the inquiring media? If such a thing happened, Yasmeena might succeed in doing something she had tried several times before. Yasmeena might commit suicide. I felt it important to give the women time to heal, time to resume new lives.

There was another reason, as well. Although I am a woman of strength, I found that I could not muster the power to tell this horrific tale. I found the entire subject incredibly painful. Instead I returned to the United States and wrote the book *Princess: A True Story of Life Behind the Veil in Saudi Arabia.* I had been discussing this book with Princess Sultana since the mid-1980s, several years after I met her in Riyadh, Saudi Arabia.

I wrote other books, ten in all, but even as I wrote the nine books after *The Rape of Kuwait,* I always held thoughts and images of Yasmeena in my mind. I never forgot her, or Lana, or the other raped women.

I don't have answers to all my questions, but I do know these things:

The women in the baby villa birthed their babies after the Kuwait government decreed that the raped women would not be allowed abortions. And so I know that Yasmeena gave birth to the Captain's baby. I learned through a friend in the Kuwaiti government that the baby was a boy. I was told that the boy was turned in to be raised at an orphanage, as were most of the babies born of those war rapes.

But what happened to Yasmeena after she gave birth? Did she return to Lebanon to her loving family? I was told that Yasmeena left Kuwait three weeks after giving birth and that her flight was to Beirut. So I feel that she did return to her family.

Did Yasmeena attempt to gain entry into Israel? I think not, because I believe that Yasmeena did not mean the words she said when she claimed to hate all things Arab and expressed her shocking wish to become a Jew. Yasmeena was speaking from the depth of her wound.

Yasmeena was such a formidable woman that I have often wondered if perhaps she sought personal revenge upon her rapist, the Captain. After all, she claimed to know his real name and the name of his village in Iraq. I have had visions of the powerful Yasmeena tracking the Captain to his village and seeking personal revenge for the horrific acts he committed against her, and other women.

Beginning in 2010, I felt even more haunted by the memory of Yasmeena and Lana. I brushed those thoughts aside, thinking that I would never find the strength to relive the stories I was told.

Then one day I sat in front of my computer to continue writing my personal story of my many adventures saving animals from torture and abuse. Something made me open a new file and I began to write about a subject I had no intention of writing about. I surprised myself when I automatically began to write about a Lebanese woman named Yasmeena. The memory of all that Yasmeena had told me felt as keen and fresh as the day I had met her. My fingers flew across the keyboard, the story pouring from me, much in the same way Yasmeena's story gushed from her on that day in Kuwait City.

My wish is that Yasmeena returned to Lebanon to reunite with her family. My wish is that Yasmeena fell in love and married. My wish is that Yasmeena is now the mother of children she loves. My wish is that Yasmeena is living a good life and that she has learned to emotionally cope with the horrors she endured in the prison circus in Kuwait City.

My wish is that Yasmeena will see this book in a bookstore in Lebanon and that she will know that she was never forgotten by this writer, and now the world.

Jean Sasson

July 2013

Homeless doggie "Kuwait" gets a home with American soldiers.

Jean Sasson visited the American soldiers stationed in the deserts of Kuwait.

Grieving father whose son was murdered by the Iraqis. His son was a resistance fighter.

Ordinary Kuwaiti's, even those accustomed to lives of ease and comfort, became fierce resistance fighters when the Iraqi army invaded. This young man is one of those heroes.

A young resistance fighter who was caught and murdered by Iraqis.
(c) The Sasson Corporation
This photo is the property of The Sasson Corporation and is not to be duplicated or
reprinted without permission.

Here are two of the happiest women I met. Both had survived a ghastly imprisonment in one of Iraq's notorious prisons. They were returned from Iraq when the war ended.

(c) The Sasson Corporation

This photo is the property of The Sasson Corporation and is not to be duplicated or reprinted without permission.

Only one of many Kuwaiti's who were maimed during torture. This banker stood firm when Iraqi soldiers tried to force him to open the bank vault. When he refused, they started cutting off his fingers, one after the other.

Perhaps Lana's body was buried in an unmarked grave in one of the many graves dug for multiple burials of Kuwaitis murdered by Iraqi soldiers.

Author Jean Sasson remained in Kuwait for three weeks after the
FREEDOM FLIGHT returned to Washington, DC. The day she was to
depart Kuwait for Riyadh, Saudi Arabia, the oil fires prevented flights.
A couple of hot-shot British pilots decided to leave and passed the
word to the author to "come on, we'll take to you Riyadh." Jean
jumped at the chance and joined the flight crew. Later she realized
that had the plane crashed (due to the blackened skies) no one would
have known she was on the flight.

The Author set to depart Kuwait on a forbidden flight.

Appendix A: War Rape

I did not write a book about Iraq or Kuwait. I wrote a book about men and women and war and rape. Rape has occurred to other women in other conflicts, and, in fact, rape as a by-product or instrument of war occurs more frequently than we like to admit. Rape of females during armed conflict goes back to the beginning of civilization. Even as I write these words, many girls and women all over the world are suffering from rape, torture and forced pregnancies. Although boys and men are raped too, women are more often the victims of this crime and there are added impediments for raped and pregnant women.

Rape is a sensitive issue in every country. It is the most intimate of crimes, violating all that humanity holds dear, including the care and protection of daughters, wives, mothers and sisters. But the crime of rape is a particularly delicate subject in the Muslim world where female virginity is protected by religion, custom and culture. The entire community keeps guard on the chastity of their females.

Also there is a second dangerous complication for the rape victims when they are often blamed for being raped. In many instances, rape victims survive the rape, yet do not survive violent reactions from family and community. Some victims may be imprisoned, or even murdered. This is under the cruel pretext of an honor crime when the family believes they cannot face the criticism of the community and that other members of the family will be dishonored if the raped woman is allowed to live.

For these reasons, any writer who reveals the stories of rape victims must take extraordinary precautions to protect the victims.

Just so we do not forget there have been many infamous war rape crimes, including China in WWII, Germany after WWII, Bosnia, Africa, and Iraq. Unless the psyche of the human male during war changes dramatically, there will be many other innocent women subjected to the brutality of war rape.

This story is timeless because there are thousands of women who are at this moment suffering the same kind of brutalities as Yasmeena and Lana suffered.

Pray for them.

Appendix B: A word from Iraqi Mayada Al-Askari

My name is Mayada Al-Askari, and my life was featured in the book, *Mayada, Daughter of Iraq.*

I am a full Iraqi, born into two prominent and well-known Iraqi families. My paternal grandfather was General Jafar Pasha Al-Askari, a brilliant man who served five times as the Iraqi Minister of Defense, the Prime Minister and was the Iraqi Minister to London twice. He was a Baghdadi who was educated at the Turkish Military College in Constantinople. While living in London and serving as the Iraqi Minister to London, he also read for the English Bar. During World War I, my grandfather won many honors for his military abilities, including the German Iron Cross, as well as the Companionship of St. Michael and St. George decorations from the British, presented directly to him by the famous General Allenby. My grandfather had first fought on the side of the Germans and Turks until many of his friends were cruelly murdered by the Sultan of the Ottoman Empire. At that time, he was convinced to move to the side of the British and to fight to free Arab nations from the grip of the Ottoman Empire, who had so brutally ruled over Arab lands for 500 long years. At the time of his tragic early death by assassination, my grandfather's obituary was written by Sir Winston Churchill.

My maternal grandfather was Sati Al-Husri who was so intellectually gifted that he graduated two full years of school for each year he attended. He graduated from Istanbul's Royal Shahany School, one of the most exclusive schools in the region, receiving his B.A. in political science. By this time, his fame as an intellectual giant had reached the ear of the Sultan of the Ottoman Empire, and my grandfather, a very young man at the time, was appointed governor of Bayna and of Koniya in Yugoslavia. He was also personally selected by the Sultan to head the educational system of the Ottoman Empire.

My grandfather was so successful in his educational endeavors that after the fall of the Sultan, he was also honored by the new president of modern Turkey, Mustafa Kemal Ataturk, who often repeated, "My only desire is to rule Turkey with the same excellence that Sati Al-Husri administered his schools".

As the years passed, my Grandfather Sati became known as the number one Arab nationalist, always believing that the Arab lands should rule themselves rather than be subjected to rule by foreign occupiers. Grandfather Sati was a famous writer and his writings live to this day. Rarely have I visited an Arab country that had not named streets or schools for my famous grandfather.

In those days when my country was ruled by the Sultan, prominent Iraqis were educated in Turkey, but their hearts were with their homeland of Mesopotamia. Upon the defeat of the Ottomans in WWI, the newly formed and named country of Iraq appeared on world maps. My grandfathers were elated, for all they wanted was freedom and trustworthy self-government for their country. As such, both were devoted to serving King Faisal I, who was appointed the King of Iraq. While Grandfather Jafar Pasha dealt with military and government matters, Grandfather Sati was involved in all aspects of the education system, as well as saving the antiquities of our ancient land.

Sadly enough, we all know now that Iraq and Iraqis have travelled a rough road from that first shining moment, from assassinations to violent government upheavals to dictators to foreign occupation. In fact, my

Grandfather Jafar Pasha was one of the first to be assassinated by rogue military officers, setting the country on a violent path.

I love my country. I love my countrymen and countrywomen. But I know that many mistakes have been made, and that many brutalities have occurred, not only against some of our Iraqi neighbors, but most often, brutalities committed by Iraqis upon other Iraqis. Under the regime of Saddam Hussein, I cannot deny that there were many innocent Iraqis tortured and murdered. I personally saw the inside of an Iraqi prison when I was arrested on false charges and directly witnessed the cruelties that Iraqi guards committed upon innocent women. Had Saddam not had affection for the teachings of self-rule by my maternal grandfather Sati Al-Husri, and responded favorably to Sati's daughter, Salwa, who was my mother, I, too, might have perished in an Iraqi prison.

And so, when my friend, Jean Sasson confided that she was writing a book that might concern me, a book about the women captured in Kuwait and held as sex prisoners by Iraqi soldiers, she asked that I read the book. If I agreed with her that the crime of war rape should receive more attention, no matter who committed the crime, she asked if I might make a comment. The fact that I am an Iraqi who loves my country would make my opinion most important, according to Jean.

For several reasons, I did not hesitate for one second. I sincerely love Jean Sasson as my dearest friend in the world. She is like family to me and has been since I first met her in 1998 when she travelled into Iraq to see for herself the devastating effects of the U.N. sanctions against Iraqi citizens. She has been a good friend, an honest friend, for many years. I also admire Jean's abilities as an author. She tackles stories about non-celebrities that few authors consider important, yet Jean has always told me that every human being living should have a voice, and have the right for their stories to be known. She is a humanist, caring for all human beings, whether male, female, adult or child. I have personally witnessed Jean's sympathetic actions in the hospitals of Iraq when she visited my country in July 1998, where small children were dying only because Iraqi doctors had no access to medicines due to the U.N. sanctions.

I know that Jean truly cares about every suffering human being and would like to right all wrongs.

Indeed, Jean was correct that such a story about Iraqi soldiers kidnapping and raping women during the occupation of Kuwait troubled me. Admittedly, I dreaded reading the true stories of the indignities inflicted upon women being held captive in Kuwait, and by men from my own beloved country. Yet I knew that Jean would write the truth that she had learned during her time in Kuwait meeting with the women. I also understood from my time in prison that some men can be exceptionally cruel. Nationality has no effect on this crime. I also understood that in times of war, there are some men who consider females to be the fruits of war, there for the taking. This occurs in every war and from men of every nation. There are no exceptions. For this reason, I agree with Jean that this story should be told, and that the world of nations should come together to work against this universal scourge against women.

Although this particular story is about how men of my own beloved nation used their power to subdue and to harm women, I believe that no exceptions can be made and that the men of my own country should be punished, as should all men who commit such brutal crimes, whether those men are Iraqi, American, British, Kuwaiti, or any man from any country in the world.

In my opinion, this heartbreaking story is one that every adult should read, regardless of their nationality.

I believe that *Yasmeena's Choice: A True Story of War, Rape, Courage and Survival* is an important and unforgettable book. I honestly believe that all feeling and thinking people will agree with me.

Mayada Al-Askari
July 2013

Mayada Al-Askari is a reporter with the highly respected GULF NEWS *newspaper in Dubai. She was featured in the book,* Mayada, Daughter of Iraq, *focusing on her time in a notorious prison in Iraq. Ms. Al-Askari has recently written the non-fiction book,* "In the King's Garden". *This book tells many compelling personal stories of Iraq from the day of its formation, Mayada's distinguished family, plus interesting and true stories about the royal family of Iraq.*

Appendix C: About Kuwaiti Soud a. Al-Mutawa

I'd like to introduce my readers to Soud a. Al-Mutawa. Soud is a very dignified Kuwaiti who makes his living working in the Kuwait banking system. He is an attractive and friendly individual who was in Kuwait with his wife and small children on August 2, 1990 when the country was invaded. All remained in Kuwait during the entire occupation. When Kuwait was freed on February 26, 1991, Soud was relieved and happy that he and his family had lived through an extremely dangerous military invasion and occupation. Many Kuwaitis were not so fortunate.

Soon after Kuwait was freed, Kuwaiti government officials, journalists and writers arrived in Kuwait on The Freedom Flight from the United States. On this occasion, some Kuwaitis were asked to volunteer their time to take Kuwait's foreign visitors around the battered land so that they might see the destruction for themselves, and to meet victims of the occupation. That's when Soud was assigned to escort me around the country. A second volunteer, a young female student named Muna, was to accompany us. When I met Soud, and later, Muna, I instinctively felt myself in good hands. Both appeared very gracious and wholly knowledgeable of all that had happened inside Kuwait during the long months of occupation.

In fact, many Kuwaitis eagerly volunteered to help as guides, wanting journalists and writers from all over the world to witness and hear from survivors what happened to ordinary Kuwaitis during that calamitous time. The Kuwaitis I met appeared hopeful that the truth of the occupation would create worldwide understanding of the brutalities of military occupations, and possibly help to prevent future wars.

During the three weeks I was in Kuwait, Soud and Muna made huge efforts to ensure that I was aware of the crimes against Kuwait and Kuwaitis. Soud, in particular, took charge as so to guarantee that I met with many Kuwaitis and understood their individual stories. And so I meet many survivors. The people I met, and the stories they told, were so vivid that even after the passage of many years, I intensely recall the people and the personal ordeals they shared with me.

Soud escorted me to meet with individual Kuwaitis whose sons had been tortured and killed for being a part of the resistance against the occupiers. Soud initiated other meetings with Kuwaitis who had been kidnapped and taken away to be imprisoned in Iraq. Soud introduced me to physicians and nurses who had been inside the country during the entire occupation, people who had personally witnessed the horrific wounds inflicted upon Kuwaitis, and who had tagged the dead and executed. He even transported me to the cemeteries where endless rows of mass graves were visible for all to see. Soud waited with me at the Shiakhan Al-Farise Hall in Surra, Kuwait where 1,000 Kuwaiti POW's were returned to their country and we witnessed the joy of reunions and the heartbreak of families who waited in vain. (Note: We must never forget that 605 Kuwaitis, taken illegally as prisoners of war on the last day of the occupation, have never been returned to their families.)

When the opportunity presented itself for us to drive into Southern Iraq, I was eager to go. I suspected that Soud might say no, since he was responsible for my safety. To my astonishment, he was as eager to make that adventurous trip slipping unauthorized into Southern

Iraq. We were told more than once by the American military to leave the area, that it was incredibly dangerous to be outside of Kuwait City, but I found Soud matched my own daring temperament, so we kept returning until the American military accepted our being there, even offering us a glass of tea and a sit-down visit. That's when we were able to meet with Iraqi people who were hoping that Saddam's government would fall, for they, too, had suffered greatly under the dictator's rule.

On the return trip from Iraq to Kuwait, we paused along the way to spend time with worried refugees stranded on the Kuwaiti/Iraqi border. We heard exploding ordinance, for there were many landmines scattered throughout the cities and the countryside, making any trip dangerous. In the refugee camp we met panicky parents and despairing children. I even rescued an abandoned puppy who was suffering from neglect. Over Soud's objections, I insisted that the dog ride with us back into Kuwait. Soud did not appear very enamored over a puppy traveling in his automobile. I had given the puppy the name "Kuwait", and was worrying Soud with my heavy sighs and concerns as to where the puppy might live since I was staying in a hotel. For sure, Soud was not going to offer the puppy a home. But along the route back into Kuwait City, we detected an American military desert camp and stopped to see what might be going on with those men. Those soldiers were stunned but delighted to meet up with an American woman in the middle of the desert between Kuwait and Iraq, and to greet a Kuwaiti survivor, for they had not been allowed into Kuwait City. Those young soldiers were happy to hear that I had named the pup "Kuwait", and on the spot they gathered around the poor pup, saying he would be their mascot and that they would take him to Germany when they were flown out of the country the following week. And so, we left "Kuwait the pup" with the American soldiers. I could see that Soud was very pleased to have someone else assume responsibility for the puppy.

Another exciting day occurred when we traveled to the desert outside Kuwait City and met other members of the American military and even ate some of their food, the MRE's the world hears about. Soud, along with the soldiers, appeared stupefied when I expressed extreme excitement over those MRE's until I confided between gulps of food that I had eaten only cookies and candy since I arrived in the country. The hotel did not yet have electricity or water; therefore, they had not opened up their restaurant. Also, there was nowhere to cook any food. I had been eating only snacks that I had packed to pass along to Kuwaiti children. Truthfully, I had been extremely hungry much of the ten days I had spent in the country. Soud was bewildered that I had been going hungry and said he would make arrangements for me to have food, for most Kuwaiti citizens had stockpiled food and would be happy to share with me. I shook my head in disbelief for I had purposefully not asked anyone in the country for food, believing that the Kuwaitis must be short on supplies.

Later, Soud introduced me to a banker he knew, a quiet but brave man who had bravely endured his fingers being cut from his hand, until he had no choice but to open up the banking safe.

One of our most touching moments was to meet the handicapped children of a home especially built for them. During the occupation, those children, along with their caretakers, had been forced to vacate their safe dwelling. Fiercely protected by the staff, all the children survived. While visiting the home with the main official of the organization, we inspected every floor of the four or five-story building, noting the damage left behind by the occupiers. While standing on the roof of the building, we heard suspicious noises. During those early days after Kuwaiti liberation, we had heard that it was not unusual for one of the Iraqi soldiers to be hidden in various buildings, for some had missed their army's exit from Kuwait. Soud and the Kuwaiti owner & administrator of the children's home seemed amazed and then amused that I did not run away, but instead armed myself with a long metal pole and rushed to the direction of the noise. We were a good unit, for Soud was immediately by my side, ready to fight, too. Thankfully we found no Iraqi soldiers to fight, although I believe we would have been a formidable team.

I especially enjoyed meeting members of the Kuwaiti resistance, for, by that time, I had met fathers and brothers who had lost their sons and siblings to the occupying army. I was happy to witness our celebrations and doubly surprised to see that the fighters had copies of my book, *The Rape of Kuwait*.

One of the most heart-rending visits occurred toward the end of my time in Kuwait. Soud was told by a member of the government that I was the only writer to be given access to the home for women who had been raped and made pregnant by the occupiers. I supposed that was my reward for writing *The Rape of Kuwait*, the only book that told the stories of Kuwaitis and others who had escaped the country after the invasion and occupation. That was a haunting visit, for those women were the only people in Kuwait who could not find something to rejoice about—their sadness was contagious and Soud and I both were devastated by their personal dilemmas. Those are the true stories you will learn about in this book.

There were many other adventures during those weeks, far too many to name, including a very sad tour of the "Highway of Death" road out of Kuwait leading back to Iraq where we saw evidence of massive death.

During those many weeks in Kuwait and my time with Soud, I believe that he came to see that I was not there only for a story. For my whole life I've been a true "people person" and I truly cared about the suffering Kuwaitis and others who had been adversely affected by the Iraqi invasion and occupation.

After I left Kuwait, I mailed Soud copies of the photographs I had taken. Soud and I made contact from time to time, and he told me that he took out my photographs frequently to relive those tragic, yet exciting times. I've never lost interest in Soud, his family, or other Kuwaitis I met. But as the years passed, we lost touch.

Last year, I made contact with Soud once again. I wanted to know how that brave young man was doing, and how his large family was faring. I was happy to hear all were well, yet surprised to learn that Soud and his wife are proud grandparents. For me, brave Soud will be forever young. I requested and received photographs of Soud's beautiful family from his wife and daughter.

Not long ago, I contacted Soud once again. On this occasion I had a few questions about the pregnant women we had met in the villa. There were several points that were unclear to me and Soud helped to rekindle my memory.

I instinctively felt that Soud would rather I not approach this subject for several reasons: The years have passed and most Kuwaitis have moved on to restore their country and heal. Most importantly, rape is a very sensitive topic, and particularly so in the Muslim world. While I know it is painful to relive those days of horror and loss, I feel strongly that this important story should not be ignored, despite the fact I was unable to write the accounts for many years.

Yet Soud graciously wished me well, for he knew that during Kuwait's time of need, I was a good friend to Kuwait and to Kuwaitis. No Kuwaiti who met me in those dark days, would say that this is not so.

Appendix D: Kuwait – A Chronology

1600s: The area now known to the world as Kuwait, which is the North-east portion of Arabian peninsula, becomes a part of the vast Ottoman Empire.

1700s: Settlers from the interior of the Arabian peninsula travel to the site of present-day Kuwait City. The settlement struggles but slowly grows into a busy trading hub.

1756: One specific family, the Al-Sabah family, gains control of the area. Over time, the Al-Sabah's managed to make an agreement with the rulers of the Ottoman Empire for semi-autonomy.

1899: Sheikh Mubarak "the Great" is an extremely strong ruler and he fights to end Kuwait's relationship with the Ottoman Empire. He arranges an agreement with Great Britain to become a protectorate of the little kingdom. In exchange for naval protection, Britain is given control of Kuwait's foreign affairs.

1937: Oil reserves are discovered by the US-British Kuwait Oil Company. Before the oil industry can fully develop, World War II breaks out, delaying. But once the war ends, development of the oil industry brings great wealth to the small nation.

1951: Kuwait's citizens achieve a high standard of living due to the great wealth brought about by the oil industry.

1961 June: Kuwait proclaims independence and ends the 62-year British protectorate. Sheikh Al-Sabah becomes Emir Al-Sabah. At this same time, Kuwait joins the Arab League.

1961: Iraq startles Kuwait and Great Britain when they claim that Kuwait rightfully belongs to Iraq. When the British military intervenes, the government of Iraq withdraws their claims.

1963: The Kuwaiti government drafts a constitution and proclaims elections in order to elect a National Assembly.

1976: Emir Al-Sabah does not appreciate interference from the Assembly. He disbands the elected National Assembly.

1980: War erupts between Iraq and Iran. The Kuwaiti government is concerned about the danger of the Iranian Shiite majority so they give financial and psychological support to Saddam Hussein and Iraq. Kuwaiti citizens throw their full support behind Iraq.

1981: Emir Al-Sabah recalls the Kuwaiti National Assembly.

1985: Unrest and security problems arise in Kuwait due to the long Iraqi/Iranian war. Iran tries to create unrest in Kuwait's Shiite's minority. That's when the Kuwaiti government orders thousands of Iranian expatriates to leave Kuwait.

1986: The Kuwaiti National Assembly is disbanded once again.

1990 July: Iraqi President Saddam Hussein depleted the Iraqi treasury during the Iran/Iraq war and he calls for Kuwait to forgive all war debts. The Kuwaiti government refuses. Saddam files a complaint with OPEC. He accuses Kuwait of stealing Iraqi oil from an oil field near the Iraqi border. Saddam threatens military action.

1990 August 2: Iraq invades Kuwait. The Kuwaiti government makes it safely to Saudi Arabia where they can continue to govern from Taif, Saudi Arabia. Saddam annexes Kuwait.

1990 August/September/October: Jean Sasson travels to London, Cairo, and Taif, Saudi Arabia to meet with

Kuwaiti survivors of the August 2ndIraqi invasion. She is one of the few writers to interview the Kuwaiti Emir and Crown Prince.

1991 January 15: Jean Sasson's book, *The Rape of Kuwait,* highlighting personal experiences fleeing their country on the day of the invasion, is published in the United States. The book becomes an instant best-seller, reaching #2 on the *New York Times* bestseller list.

1991 January: The UN passes a resolution ordering Iraq to pull out of Kuwait. Saddam Hussein refuses. The United States leads the UN-backed bombing air campaign against the Iraqi military in Kuwait and Iraq.

1991 February: Saddam orders his men to set fire to the Kuwaiti oil fields. The military obeys, torching the Kuwaiti oil fields as they leave the country.

1991 February 26: The Iraqi army leaves Kuwait. Upon departure, enemy soldiers kidnap Kuwaiti citizens as hostages, taking them on the military retreat. It is believed that some Kuwaitis perished on the "Highway of Death" attack on the road leading from Kuwait. Others are imprisoned, but later returned on the orders of the UN. 605 Kuwaitis disappear forever in Saddam's prisons.

1991 February: After the Iraqi army departs, Allied forces arrive in Kuwait City. The entire country erupts into a mass celebration.

1991 March 13-16: The Kuwaiti government sponsors the **FREEDOM FLIGHT TO KUWAIT.** Author Jean Sasson is an invited guest. Jean Sasson remains in the country for three weeks after the **FREEDOM FLIGHT** returns to the USA.

1991 March: Emir Al-Sabah returns to Kuwait, calling for a three-month period of martial law.

1991 March 21: Approximately 1,000 Kuwaiti POW's are returned to Kuwait. Relatives of the missing gather at SURRA at the Shiakhan Al-Farise Hall to greet the survivors. Jean Sasson is escorted to the hall by Soud

a. Al-Mutawa, where both talk with families and survivors and commiserate with the families who wait in vain.

1992: Emir Al-Sabah allows National Assembly elections. Everyone is surprised when opposition candidates win many votes.

1993: The UN establishes a new Kuwait-Iraq border. Saddam orders Iraqi border raids into Kuwait. The United States dispatches American troops.

1994: The UN puts pressure on Iraq to formally recognize Kuwait's independence and the new UN-defined borders.

1999: After elections, government supporters and the Al-Sabah family are dismayed when Islamists dominate the new assembly.

2000: Over the years, the Kuwaiti government, along with a special committee, calls for action regarding the 605 missing Kuwaitis still believed to be in Iraq. The Iraqi government denies all, but the families know that their family members are either in Iraqi prisons or have been murdered by the Iraqi regime. One of the missing is Fayeq Abdul Jaleel (the pen name of Fayeq Al-Ayadhi) who is a famous Arab poet known throughout the Muslim world and beyond. Jaleel's son, Fares AL-Ayadhi, never gave up on his father and searched until Fayeq's remains were found in a mass grave in the deserts of Iraq. Fares is in the process of writing a book about his father's life, a man who gave his life for his country. (Fares' father was one of the more active members of the men fighting for Kuwait and was captured prior to the retreat of the Iraqi army.)

2000: A death sentence is given to Kuwait's pro-Iraqi puppet ruler from the days of the 1990 invasion and occupation.

2001: Kuwaiti courts commute the death sentence to life for the pro-Iraqi puppet ruler, much to the dismay of many Kuwaiti citizens.

2002 March: Many thousands of soldiers congregate on the Kuwait-Iraq border for a US-led military campaign to oust Iraqi leader Saddam Hussein.

2003: Emir Al-Sabah appoints Sheikh Sabah al-Ahmad al-Sabah Prime Minister. (This has never happened before, signifying a division of powers.)

2005 January: Violence erupts between Islamist militants and police, spreading alarm throughout the country.

2005 May: Parliament passes a law so that Kuwaiti women can vote and run for parliament.

2005 June: Massouma al-Mubarak is appointed as the first female cabinet minister.

2006 January: Emir Sheikh Jaber dies. Crown Prince Sheikh Saad succeeds to the throne but poor health creates a government crisis and he is forced to resign. Sheikh Sabah al-Ahmad becomes the new Emir.

2006 April: Women cast their votes for the first time in an election, but later fail to win any seats in the parliamentary elections.

2006: Mass graves are discovered in Iraq. Many of the dead are identified as missing Kuwaitis (by DNA).

2007 July: Kuwaitis are shocked when they are told to conserve electricity. Their own generators struggle to meet demands of economic growth fueled by record oil exports.

2008 March: There is discord in the government. The Emir dissolves opposition-dominated parliament. He calls for elections in May after cabinet resigns.

2008 May: The Emir calls for elections when his cabinet resigns. Still, no women are elected although Islamists win more than half of the 50 seats.

2009 January: Prime Minister Sheikh Nasser Mohammad al-Ahmad al-Sabah forms a new government after chaos in the Parliament when a Shiite cleric visits.

2009 February: Kuwaiti citizens are surprised when Kuwait's Foreign Minister visits Baghdad for a high level visit, the first formal meetings between the two governments since Iraq invaded Kuwait in 1990.

2009 May: Kuwaiti women make history when three of their number wins seats in the Parliament.

2009 October: Kuwaiti women celebrate when the Constitutional Court makes a ruling that Kuwaiti women will be allowed to obtain passports without the consent of their husbands. Another ruling says that female MPs are not required to wear an Islamic head cover when working. The ruling puts Kuwait in the forefront of women's rights in the region.

2009 December: The Prime Minister survives an attempt by the opposition to remove him over corruption allegations.

2011 March: Inspired by protests around the Arab world, many young people in Kuwait demonstrate for reform.

2011 December: There are protests over government corruption. The Emir dissolves the parliament.

2012 January 22: Sheikh Saud Al-Sabah passed away after a long battle with cancer at the age of 68, the Emiri Diwan announced. The Sheikh was a member of Kuwait's royal family and vigorously served as Kuwait's US Ambassador and he was the leading voice calling for international help after Iraq's invasion and occupation. He was laid to rest in Kuwait.

2012 February: The Islamist-led opposition takes control of the Kuwaiti parliament due to a wave of public anger over political deadlock. The Emir asks the outgoing Prime Minster to form a new cabinet. .

2012 May: The Emir blocks a proposal by MPs to make all legislation comply with Islamic law.

2012 June: The Emir suspends parliament. Kuwait's highest court annuls the election results, reinstating the previous assembly.

2012 October: The Emir once again dissolves parliament for the fifth time in six years. Thousands rally against possible changes to the election law. Kuwaitis are shocked when a prominent opposition figure breaks a taboo by directly criticizing the Emir. The Emir orders changes to the election laws, reducing the number of votes per citizen in parliamentary elections from four votes, to one vote. The opposition then calls for an election boycott. Tens of thousands of people march against the new voting rules. The crowd is dispersed by tear gas and stun grenades.

2012 November: Thousands of protestors march on the prison where the opposition figure is held for insulting the emir. The police rout the crowd with tear gas. The emir stands firm.

2012 December: Kuwaitis vote in a parliamentary election held under the new polling rules. Turnout is low.

2013 June: The Kuwaiti Constitutional Court scrapped the parliamentary election of December 2012, but approved the Emir's electoral law that created the boycott. The court has called for a new election to replace the current parliament.

Despite the recent political upheavals, most observers agree that Kuwait has one of the most lively parliaments and freest media in the Middle East.

Appendix E: Iraq – A Chronology

1534–1918: Region now known as Iraqi is part of the Ottoman Empire.

1920: San Remo Peace Conference of Allied Powers endorses the British and French mandate over the Middle East.

1921: King Faisal is crowned King of Iraq.

1927: British strike oil at Kirkuk, Iraq.

1932: Formal independence is given to Iraq

1933: King Faisal I dies of natural causes. His son, Ghazi, is crowned king.

1936: Jafar Pasha Al-Askari, Minister of Defense, is assassinated during Iraq's first military coup. His death is an enormous loss for the newly founded country.

1938: Jafar Pasha Al-Askari's brother-in-law and best friend, Nouri Pasha Al-Said becomes Iraq's Prime Minister

1939: King Ghazi I dies in an automobile accident. His four-year-old son, Faisal II, succeeds. Prince Abd al-llah is appointed Regent.

1941: There is a military coup and Iraq's king and Prime Minister is forced to temporarily flee.

1958: Another military coup has more tragic results. The Prime Minister and members of the royal family, including the king, are assassinated.

1959: Yet another coup. This is when Saddam Hussein has to flee to Egypt.

1968: The Baathists return to power and Saddam Hussein becomes second in command.

1979: Saddam Hussein becomes president. One of his first presidential acts is to purge many members of the Baathist Party.

1980: Iraq and Iran go to war.

1981: Israel bombs the Iraqi Osirak nuclear plant near Baghdad.

1987: Saddam Hussein uses chemical warfare against Kurdish villages, killing thousands. The world ignores the inhumane act.

1988 February: Formal cease-fire in the Iran-Iraq war.

1990 August: Iraq invades Kuwait. UN Resolution 660 calls for Saddam Hussein to withdrawn his troops. Iraq annexes Kuwait as its nineteenth province.

1991 January 17: Operation Desert Storm begins.

1991 February: Iraqi troops are routed.

1991 February 28: There is a ceasefire.

1991 Mid-March/early April: Southern Shiite and northern Kurdish populations are encouraged by Iraq defeat. They rebel against Saddam, resulting in a brutal crackdown.

1991 April 3: The UN Security Council Resolution 687 establishes the terms of the peace. All Iraqi troops are out of Kuwait.

1991 April: UN-approved safe-haven established in northern Iraq to protect the Kurds. Iraq ordered to end all military activity in the area.

1992 August: A no-fly zone is set up in southern Iraq. Iraqi military planes are forbidden to enter.

1998 June: American author, Jean Sasson, (who wrote *The Rape of Kuwait*) writes to Saddam Hussein requesting permission and a visit visa to go into Iraq. A formal invitation is issued from Saddam Hussein's office.

1998 July/August: Jean Sasson obtains her Iraqi visa from the UN Mission in NY. She travels to Jordan and from there goes by automobile into Baghdad, remaining in the country on a research trip for three weeks.

1998 November: All UN inspectors withdraw from Iraq.

2002 September: President George Bush calls for action against Iraq. Iraq agrees to allow international weapons inspectors to return to Iraq without conditions.

2002 November: UN weapons inspectors return to Iraq backed by a UN resolution which threatens serious consequences if Iraq is found to be in "breach" of its terms.

2003 March: UK's ambassador to the UN says the diplomatic process on Iraq has ended. The arms inspectors evacuate. US President George W Bush gives Saddam Hussein and his sons 48 hours to leave Iraq or face war. Saddam and his sons ignore the order.

March 19 2003: US-led invasion leads to the end of Saddam Hussein's government, marks start of years of violent conflict with different groups competing for power.

2003 July: US appointed Governing Council meets for first time. Commander of US forces says his troops face low-intensity guerrilla-style war. Saddam's sons Uday and Qusay, along with Qusay's young son, are killed in gun battle in Mosul.

2003 August: Suicide truck bomb wrecks UN headquarters in Baghdad. Popular UN envoy, Sergio Vieira de Mello, is killed in the attack.

2003 December 14: Saddam Hussein is captured in Tikrit.

2004 April/May: Shiite militias loyal to radical cleric Moqtada Sadr start fighting against coalition forces. The US military responds and hundreds are reported killed in fighting during the month-long US military siege of the Sunni Muslim city of Fallujah.

2005 February: Eight million Iraqis freely vote in elections for a Transitional National Assembly.

2005 April: Amid escalating violence, parliament selects Kurdish leader Jalal Talabani as president. Ibrahim Jaafari, a Shiite, is named as prime minister.

2005 June: Massoud Barzani is sworn in as regional president of Iraqi Kurdistan.

2005 August: An Iraqi draft constitution is endorsed by Shiite and Kurdish negotiators. Sunni representatives reject the document.

2005 October: Iraqi voters approve a new constitution, which aims to create an Islamic federal democracy.

2005 December: Iraqis vote for the first full-term government and parliament since the American led invasion.

2006 May/June: Sectarian violence claims the lives of more than 100 Iraqi civilians a day, according to the UN.

2006 June 7: Al-Qaeda leader in Iraq, Abu Musab al-Zarqawi, is killed in an air strike.

2006 November: Iraq and Syria restore diplomatic relations after nearly a quarter century. During this same period of time, more than 200 die in car bombings in the mostly Shiite area of Sadr City in Baghdad, in the worst attack on the capital since the US-led invasion of 2003.

2006 December: Iraq Study Group report reports to President Bush on future policy in Iraq. Their report describes the situation in Iraq as grave and deteriorating.

2006 December: Saddam Hussein is executed for crimes against humanity.

2008 September: The US hands over control of the western province of Anbar. It is the first Sunni province to be returned to the Iraqi Shiite led government.

2008 November: The Iraqi Parliament approves a security pact with the United States under which all US troops are due to leave the country by the end of 2011.

2009 January: The Iraqi government takes control of security in Baghdad's fortified Green Zone, assuming more powers over foreign troops based in the country.

2009 March: President Barack Obama announces the withdrawal of most US troops by the end of 2010. An advisory force will leave by the end of 2011.

2009 June: Six years after the invasion, the US withdraws from Iraqi towns and cities, handing over security duties to new Iraqi forces.

2010 January: "Chemical" Ali Hassan al-Majid, a key figure in Saddam Hussein's government, is executed.

2010 August: Seven years after the US-led invasion, the last US combat brigade leaves Iraq.

2010 October: A church in Baghdad is seized by militants. The militants murder 52 Christians in what is described as the worst single disaster to hit Iraq's Christians in modern times.

2011 August: Violence escalates. There are more than 40 coordinated nationwide attacks in one day.

2011 December: The US military completes troop pull-out.

2012: Shiite areas are targeted throughout the country, sparking fears of a new sectarian conflict. The numbers are sobering: 200 people killed in January; 160 in June, 113 in July, 70 in August, 62 in September, and 35 in November.

2012 December: President Jalal Talabani suffers a stroke but slowly recovers.

2013: Widespread sectarian attacks continue.

Appendix F: History of Iraq's Claims to Kuwait

What is the historical background to past Iraqi government claims that Kuwait should be a part of Iraq?

At the end of World War I, there was a secret agreement between England and France when the two countries divided up the Arab world into spheres of influence. The secret agreement was called the Sikes-Picot agreement, basically making most of the Middle East into colonies for the two nations.

With a careless stroke of his pen, Great Britain's representative in the region, Sir Percy Cox, created modern Iraq. His map included the provinces of Baghdad, Basra and the Kurdish regions in the north, despite the fact the 1920 Ottoman-Allies Treaty of Sevres had promised the Kurds a country of their own. At the same time, Sir Percy Cox "created" Saudi Arabia and Kuwait. The people living in Iraq believed that their borders should have extended to the Gulf (the Shatt-al-Arab parkway), which included Kuwait.

As soon as Iraq achieved independence from England, the government made an effort to restore Kuwait to Iraq. The government of Iraq was unsuccessful.

After Kuwait became independent in 1961, Iraq's president Abd al-Karim Qassim renewed Iraq's claim to Kuwait. The British responded to the claim by sending in troops and enlisting the assistance of the Arab League. Iraq later ended its boycott of the Arab League and formally recognized Kuwaiti independence two years later, in 1963.

Although Iraq has claimed Kuwait as a part of their nation since the early days of modern Iraq, Saddam Hussein was the only Iraqi leader whose military formally occupied the small country.

The dispute continues. Several times I have heard prominent Iraqis privately complain that Kuwait should be a part of their nation. They say that the borders of Iraq and Kuwait were drawn in colonial times, by colonial powers, and that the decision for Kuwait to be a sovereign nation should not stand.

Appendix G: The Freedom Flight, the Return Flight into Kuwait after Gulf War I

Sitting in an airplane, making my way through the clouds, I am once again being carried away to meet with Kuwaitis. But on this happy day, at this ecstatic hour, memories capture my thoughts, taking me to an earlier, more somber time, in September and October, 1990. It's been over seven months since the Iraqi army burst upon the Kuwaitis, occupying and annexing the small Kuwaiti nation in a matter of hours.

It's been six months since I traveled to London, Cairo, Riyadh and Taif so that I could interview many of those people caught in Kuwait on that fateful day, a day that transformed the momentum of the entire region.

Most of the Kuwaitis I came to know through my research while writing a book about the Iraqi invasion of Kuwait had escaped the occupation after fleeing into Saudi Arabia. From there, many continued their journey to continue their days of exile in Egypt or London.

Although those I interviewed had personally evaded death, their misery was genuine, with some refugees grieving the loss of family members, and all mourning the loss of their country.

Those tragic personal stories became a part of the small tome *The Rape of Kuwait*. When it was published in January 1991, the book became an instant best-seller, reaching #2 on the *New York Times* bestseller list. While *Rape* revealed the stories of Kuwaitis who had survived the invasion, I am now interested in learning what had happened to those Kuwaitis who had remained in Kuwait during the seven- month occupation. I have been thinking about them for a long time, and had read every newspaper article I could find on the occupation, as well as watch endless television shows featuring the events in Iraq and Kuwait.

Numerous media reports regarding robbery, rape and murder give me reason to believe that the Kuwaitis who remained in the occupied land met with endless life-threatening challenges. I often ask myself: what dark stories are the Kuwaitis holding on to, ready to share with the world? I will know soon enough for my plan is to remain inside the war-battered country after most passengers on the Freedom Flight return to the United States. I've packed my bags for a four-week stay, although I might remain for a shorter or longer period, according to the situation on the ground.

After the Allied Armies successfully wrested the small Kuwaiti state from the grasp of the huge Iraqi army, the Freedom Flight was organized by the Embassy of the State of Kuwait. This is the first official trip into the country. I'm sure the Kuwaiti government arranged this trip for several reasons. From what I have been told, the country was devastated. The government wants to rebuild the destroyed infrastructure as soon as possible. But there is a second, equally important reason for the trip. The government and people of Kuwait want to demonstrate to the world precisely what human rights violations transpired during the long months of occupation.

And who can blame them? The government and the people deserve justice.

I've been personally absorbed with all things Kuwaiti and Iraqi for the past seven months, so I am pleased to be included on the journey. After settling into my seat, I walk through the plane, searching for familiar faces. I know that there are 146 passengers plus crew onboard because I have counted the hosts and the guests listed on the official guest list.

While I have twice met the Kuwaiti Ambassador to the United States, His Excellency Sheikh Saud Nasir Al-Sabah, I see only a few others that I recognize, including Robert Mosbacher, the Secretary of Commerce and his wife, Georgette, along with thirteen members of Congress from Ohio, California, Maryland, Oklahoma, Pennsylvania, Rhode Island, New York and Texas. I soon spot General Alexander Haig, a sunny-faced man who is smiling and talking with people I do not know. I remember seeing the names of Mr. Mortimer Zuckerman and Andrew Young and know that they must be in the general area. There's a host of other guests, including prominent names in the media industry as well as a large group of CEO's representing some of America's largest corporations.

I see Ambassador Al-Sabah chatting with some of his guests onboard. He is smiling, too, and obviously very pleased that his country has been freed. I am delighted for him. There's no doubt that the past seven months have been the most challenging of his life. For certain, no diplomat ever worked harder on behalf of his country.

I recall the events leading up to my first meeting with the ambassador. I had instigated the meeting when I wrote him a personal letter expressing my sorrow about the invasion. I mentioned that I lived in Saudi Arabia and was planning to meet with and interview people who had survived the first day of war and who had left the country to seek asylum in neighboring lands.

My idea to interview survivors was prompted by a combination of concern and curiosity. I had lived in the area for a long time and enjoyed a number of friendships with Arab people, so, I was genuinely concerned about what was happening to the ordinary people in Kuwait. After twelve years of living in Saudi Arabia and traveling around the area, I was capable of journeying in the area alone to interview those most affected.

But I knew I would have problems obtaining information without a specific document issued by the government of Kuwait. My personal knowledge of Arabs made me aware that few Arabs will confide important or personal matters to westerners they do not know. At least they will not do so without being told that their personal stories revelations will not displease their government. Therefore I knew that I must have a written introduction from the Kuwaiti government. This knowledge had driven me to contact the ambassador so that I might obtain that very important letter of introduction.

A few days after posting my letter, I was surprised by a telephone call from the ambassador. He telephoned me at my home in Atlanta, Georgia. During the call, he invited me to come to Washington. I accepted the invitation and arrived in the city a few days later.

The Ambassador was very accommodating and gracious, providing me with a formal letter stating that any Kuwaiti who felt compelled to tell me about their experiences, should feel free to do so. There were no instructions for the Kuwaitis as to what they should or should not confide.

After living in a Middle Eastern land where the government insists upon controlling every aspect of life, including everything to be released in the media, I was pleased and relieved to discover that the Kuwait rulers were different. From the letter I was given, it was clear that there was not going to be any official interference. The Kuwaitis I would meet and interview would be free to tell me anything that didn't make them personally uncomfortable.

Although the Ambassador was a gentleman, he was all business, so I was surprised when he worriedly confided a personal matter. He told me that wife and some of his children had returned to Kuwait a few weeks previous to the invasion. Out of fear for their lives, they were living under assumed names. He was hoping to have them brought out of the country soon. I felt so badly for his situation. Not only was he deeply troubled for the well-being of his country, he had good reason to be worried over the welfare of his family.

The Ambassador failed to reveal that he was married to the daughter of the emir. Later when I learned that his wife was the emir's daughter, I understood even better that their circumstances could easily turn dire. The Ambassador was protective of his country and highly critical of President Saddam Hussein and the attack and occupation of Kuwait. He appeared on many American television shows expressing his anger and disgust with the occupiers of his country. If Iraqi officials discovered that the outspoken ambassador's wife and children were in Kuwait, and that they were so closely related to the emir, there was considerable risk that the ambassador's family members would be taken to Iraq and imprisoned, or possibly executed.

After receiving my introduction letter, I wished the ambassador and his family well and started on my trip to the Middle East.

*It's important to note that neither the Kuwaiti ambassador nor any other official with the Kuwaiti government was involved with scheduling, control over my interviews, or assuming any costs I incurred. The Kuwaiti government never offered to pay my expenses, and I never asked. In fact, such a thing had not entered my mind, and I'm sure the same applied to the Ambassador. However, there were very Kuwaitis I met while on my journey who personally offered to help me to make contact with specific Kuwaitis who had compelling stories of escape. I accepted their assistance in making introductions, a common procedure for any writer or journalist.

The research/interview trip was a success only because Kuwaitis were keen to tell their harrowing stories. After interviewing Kuwaitis in London I traveled to Egypt, where I was met by my ex-husband Peter Sasson and his new wife Julie. Peter and I had been married for ten years and after our divorce remained close friends. Julie and I had hit it off from our first meeting so I felt close to Peter's wife, too. Peter, who was a talented photographer, had agreed to accompany me when needed in order to take photographs, as I have no skills in that area. We were a finely tuned team, and after finishing our work in Cairo, the three of us flew into Riyadh.

I operated out of Peter and Julie's villa while in Riyadh, although I spent most of my days at the Kuwaiti Embassy since it was difficult to connect with Kuwaitis who were scattered all over Saudi Arabia. Riyadh was a huge city and the Kuwaitis were living in housing in various areas. Lucky for me, most Kuwaitis made frequent visits to their Embassy officials to find out what might be happening in their homeland.

I spent many hours of the day and night with the homeless Kuwaitis, commiserating with them as they despaired of their losses. Before long I was travelling about with the female Kuwaiti refugees and exploring the housing the Saudi government made available. I also visited the schools quickly formed for the Kuwaiti children.

The Saudi government was an excellent host. I'm sure that the royal family had never forgotten that one hundred years before, the ruling Kuwaiti monarch had provided sanctuary to Saudi Arabia's first king, Abdul Aziz, in the days before he became king. Abdul Aziz was a young man in exile in Kuwait with his father in the early 1900's, before he fought and defeated the Rashid's, winning back Saudi Arabia for his family. His sons were still ruling in Saudi Arabia, and by their hospitality, they showed that they had never forgotten that it was the Al-Sabah family who made it possible for their own father to regain control of Saudi Arabia.

There was only one problem. All the Kuwaiti women I met hated being in Saudi Arabia. For the most part, the Kuwaiti women were educated and accustomed to personal freedoms. In Kuwait they drove their own automobiles to school, work, or shopping. They lived much freer lives than their Saudi sisters who were generally guarded by a male relative and had little freedom outside their home. And, most alarming to my Kuwaiti female friends, they were not accustomed to roving mutawas, or religious clerics. Those stern-faced men were extremely active during a time when the kingdom was overrun with Arab women accustomed to freedom.

They took the greatest pleasure in harassing women, inspecting their attire and screaming insults to those not wearing the face veil and abaaya.

After living in one of the country's most conservative cities for many years, I was accustomed to being alert for those sharp-eyed men so obsessed with making sure women dressed and behaved moderately. While Kuwaiti women dressed modestly, many of them had never veiled. But those Saudi clerics were determined to remake the Kuwaiti women to their liking.

Since my fair coloring and blonde hair obviously marked me as a foreigner from Europe or America, the religious authorities generally ignored me. Several times I was amused to find Kuwaiti women hiding behind me when we were approached by the Saudi clerics. Those poor women would be whispering in my ear, "Keep walking," or "Help me. Hide me, Jean."

Afterward they would be sweating from stress and claiming they were ready to go and fight the Iraqi army by themselves if that would get them out of Saudi Arabia.

They found it difficult to believe that I lived happily in conservative Riyadh for twelve years and often joked with me as they questioned *my* sanity.

There *was* a world of difference between the Kuwaiti life and the Saudi life, and relations between the two groups were often strained.

While in Riyadh, I telephoned the government in exile living in Taif, Saudi Arabia, a famous mountain resort favored by those wanting to escape the heat of the desert cities. I was surprised but delighted to be invited to interview the Kuwaiti Crown Prince, and the Kuwaiti Emir.

The second time I met with the ambassador was after I had returned from my trip and after I had written the book. The book was a basic news report that only took me six weeks to write, although the timing was layered with several months of travel and interviews. The urgency of the writing shows, but it was an important record of the first day of the invasion.

The book had just come off the printing presses, and I was thrilled to present the ambassador with a copy. He smiled widely while flipping through the book. He naively asked if I had telephoned President George Bush to tell him about the book. I smiled at his question, telling him that I had never met the president and would never be put through to him at the White House. The ambassador seemed taken aback, like so many Arabs I have known who don't realize that all Americans do not enjoy personal friendships with their presidents.

*In the Middle East, the poorest citizen can request a meeting with the king, who is frequently available at desert tent meetings when he (the king) travels around the country for the purpose of meeting with citizens. The king will listen to tales of woe and pass on the petitioner to meet with one of his ministers to arrange for solutions to certain problems.

During our conversation I mentioned that I had seen a news program where American soldiers were interviewed. I was disturbed to hear one of our soldiers say that he nor his fellow soldiers understood why they were in Saudi Arabia and preparing for war to fight the Iraqis. I told the ambassador, "When I heard that soldier, I felt sorry that I was unable to put a copy of this book into his hands. I wish every soldier had a copy. Then they would know why they are where they are, and the reason behind their deployment."

The ambassador was quiet, but I could tell that he was thinking about what I had said. Then his eyes began to sparkle. He replied, "You are right, Jean. The ones being sent to fight should know exactly why they are there. They should read the personal stories. Then they will know why they have been sent to free Kuwait." The conversation gained momentum. The ambassador asked for details about my publisher, wanting the contact information. I quickly found the phone number for my publisher. The ambassador placed a call, speaking with the owner of the publishing house, asking if he might fly to Washington to meet with him.

Needless to say, I was stunned by the rapid and firm action.

The following day the publisher came to the Kuwaiti Embassy to meet with the ambassador. Before I had time to think about what might happen, the ambassador ordered 200,000 copies of *The Rape of Kuwait* to be delivered to the Kuwaiti Embassy in Washington. The Embassy hired workers to load the airplane to transport copies of my book to Saudi Arabia. I later heard that the books were given out to any and all soldiers interested in reading the personal accounts of war refugees from Kuwait.

I was impressed by the Ambassador's determination to make certain that soldiers about to fight

227

for his country knew something of why they were fighting.

Although I cannot claim friendship with Ambassador Al-Sabah, I found many reasons to admire and respect him. He was a soft- spoken, gentle man who was working with many governments so that his country might be saved from foreign occupation. Although he had been viciously attacked by various members of the American media for his efforts, I often wondered what they thought he should do differently. All critics of the ambassador's actions should have considered what they might do if someone broke into their homes, stole all their belongings, murdered their young men, raped the women, and forced all to become citizens of an invading country. The ambassador was a man diplomatically defending his country, trying with all his might to have the invaders kicked out. I thought he should be applauded rather than criticized. (*My opinion has not changed.)

Back to the Freedom Flight:

After walking around for a while, I settle once more into my seat and read until I hear that we were nearing Manama, Bahrain. We will spend the night in Bahrain and fly from there to Kuwait the following day. While on the flight we are told that plans have changed, that we will not be staying the following night in Kuwait, that it was too dangerous. There are many unexploded bombs in unexpected places, and that some Iraqi soldiers who missed returning to Iraq with their fellow soldiers have come out of hiding to threaten Kuwaitis.

I fret over this unexpected and unwelcome information. I had planned on remaining in the hotel in Kuwait after other guests departed. I don't want to make the return trip to the United States with other Freedom Flight guests. I want to explore the country for myself. I want to seek out Kuwaitis and other nationalities who remained in country during the occupation.

When we finally arrive in Kuwait, there is nothing to do about my luggage because no luggage is being unloaded from the airplane. Buses are standing by to take us on a tour of Kuwait City.

Once in Kuwait City we are met by His Highness Sheik Saud Al- Abdullah Al-Salem Al-Sabah, Crown Prince and Prime Minister. The Crown prince remembers me from six months before when I interviewed him in Taif. He appears ecstatic to see a familiar face. He's quick to tell me that he was very pleased to have a copy of the book I had written. In a sudden burst of unexpected dialog, the Crown Prince says that he must give me a gift. He would like to present me with a villa in Kuwait City, so that I might come often to visit my Kuwaiti friends. I'm so stunned I can't find words to respond. The ambassador is standing beside the Crown Prince, and he smiles but makes no comment.

I force a smile while I'm searching for a gentle manner of turning down the offer of such a generous gift. Although all the royals I have met have a habit of offering expensive gifts to those they like, the one self-imposed rule I had always followed during my years of living in the Middle East, and knowing members of the Saudi royal family, was that I never accepted presents if I could not reciprocate accordingly. While I might take a box of chocolates or a bouquet of flowers, I was always resolute in refusing expensive gifts. (The only occasion when I was unable to keep my vow was when a Kuwaiti princess slipped an expensive watch in the pocket of my coat hanging in her coat closet. I discovered the watch months later when the coat was sent to be dry cleaned. By that time I had lost touch with that particular princess and had no way of returning it.)

I keep smiling, hoping for some help from the ambassador, whom I am sure knew that writers from the west cannot accept any payments or gifts for writing a book. But the ambassador stands quietly, still smiling, leaving the decision wholly up to me.

Finally I shake my head and tell the Crown Prince, "You are too kind, but I am unable to accept such a generous gift. I do thank you, from the bottom of my heart."

Perhaps the Crown Prince knew that I would reply in such a manner because he does not appear to take offense. Many times I annoyed Saudi royals by refusing gifts, but thankfully he remains good natured, smiling his big smile and telling me that he hopes to see me again one day. But the occasion will be the last time I am in the company of Kuwait's Crown Prince.

After the brief meeting with the Crown Prince, guests of the Kuwaiti government spend a long depressing day looking at damaged buildings, destroyed palaces and homes, and being shown basements and dungeons where torture equipment is still in view. The sights and smells are ghastly and if there were any doubts, it is clear that the Kuwaitis suffered mightily and that the little country has been wholly devastated by the invaders.

The burning oil wells create the most emotion and buzz from the crowd. Some people are gasping, others speaking loudly and rapidly while others are silent, quietly studying the damage.

I observe the ambassador's wife and daughter weeping while clinging to each other. The ambassador is offering what comfort he can. I understand why they feel so sorrowful. Kuwaiti skies are dark and black curling smoke is spiraling to the heavens. Kuwaiti air is thick. The burning oil wells and heavy smoke have blocked the sun. Everything feels cold.

The sight reminds me of how a nuclear winter might appear. I am particularly saddened by the sight of birds and other creatures dying all around us. All are covered in slick black oil. They are unable to fly. They are unable to walk. They sit miserably, waiting for death.

All living things in Kuwait have suffered and are still suffering.

What an avoidable tragedy!

At the end of the day, somber guests are driven back to the airplane. Over the day I have considered my problem and planned my strategy. Once we arrive at the airport, I rush to speak with the flight crew and describe my situation, telling them that I must stay in Kuwait. But, I will need my luggage. They are extremely helpful, jumping to assist me, looking through the bags to find my seven large cases. Most people onboard had limited their luggage to small carry-on bags, so my large, heavy luggage is easily found, and quickly removed from the plane.

There are three or four other people there to see the flight off. They are Kuwaitis. While standing to wave at the passengers returning to the United States, I ask if I might catch a ride with them back into the city. They are happy to help me, despite the number and weight of my bags. Although the vehicle is crowded, everyone keeps a happy attitude because Kuwait is free once again.

As the huge airplane pulls away, I catch a sight of Ambassador Al-Sabah peering at me from his window seat. He looks so surprised to see me on the tarmac that I fear he will call for the plane to stop, believing that a passenger has been left behind. But perhaps my joyful smile and friendly wave assures him that I am doing exactly what I want to do. So he takes no action and for that I am relieved.

Jean Sasson

July 20, 2013

Appendix H: Excerpt from *The Rape of Kuwait*

The following are my earliest writings from the first drafts of a manuscript I wrote during the months of October, November and December 1990. Later my manuscript became the bestselling book, *The Rape of Kuwait: The True Story of Iraqi Atrocities Against a Civilian Population.*

*Since the book is no longer in print, I often receive questions about the book. For those who are interested, the following is information on the writing of *The Rape of Kuwait.*

Notes for the Preface:

For twelve years I made my home in the Middle East. During this time I had come to know and love the people of the area. For this reason, the recurring violence there had never failed to pain me, for I knew firsthand the very people caught up in the explosive passions that plague the region.

Many Arabs were my friends. I know them as human beings. My Arab friends grew up just as the rest of us, filled with hope, planning their futures, hoping for marriage and family. They suffer when sorrow comes into their lives. And they die. But too many Arabs died only because they were born in the most tumultuous region on earth.

After witnessing countless upheavals over the course of the last decade, I had reached the conclusion that still more wars would be fought among the Arabs. There were too many strong-willed dictators, luxury loving kings, unsolved ambitions, and plentiful instruments of death available for the region to be peaceful. The entire area was filled with restless armies, tanks, missiles, and military hardware, mostly sold to Middle Eastern countries by America, Russia and various European nations. For all these reasons, I strongly felt that the mounting tensions in the Middle East would escalate, creating more wars.

During the summer of 1990, I watched with mounting dread as Saddam Hussein, President of Iraq, launched insults at the Al-Sabah rulers of Kuwait. Saddam was very annoyed because he had borrowed an enormous amount of money from Kuwait and Saudi Arabia, money to finance the eight-year war against their common enemy, Iran. The war had not accomplished Saddam's goals, ending in a stalemate. Now a very angry Saddam was sitting in Baghdad with an army of one million soldiers, a shattered economy, and unrealized ambitions.

He had asked those governments to forgive his debts, and to give him more funds to repair his destroyed country. Now the Saudis and Kuwaitis were refusing to forgive his debt, and Saddam was furious. He felt that he had given up Iraq's oil wealth, and lost thousands of young Iraqi soldiers, for nothing.

Having read everything published about him, I feared for the Kuwaitis and the Saudis because Saddam was a strong man psychologically and his bite was as bad as his bark. I telephoned friends living in Kuwait and Dubai in the United Arab Emirates, people who had fled the Lebanese Civil War, and advised that it might be safer to return to Beirut to face the problems in that war-saddled country. My friends laughed, telling me not to worry. They believed that Saddam was bluffing. How I hoped they were right and I was wrong.

On the night of August 1, 1990, I settled in to watch one of my favorite television shows, "Nightline" hosted by Ted Koppel. Atlanta was seven hours behind Kuwait, so it was early morning in Kuwait. I was horrified to hear Mr. Koppel announce the breaking story that the Iraqi military had invaded Kuwait. The Iraqi military had invaded several hours before and were now racing toward Kuwait City, according to excited reporters.

I was aghast, but had no way of knowing that in that instant, my life was changed forever, just as the lives of Kuwaitis and Iraqis were forever altered.

In the days that followed, I was so gripped by the unfolding drama taking place in Kuwait that I found I was unable to concentrate on a half-completed manuscript on the Middle East. I listened intently to the press conferences calls by Sheik Saud Nasir Al-Sabah, the Kuwaiti Ambassador to the United States. I felt such sorrow as I heard his appeals to all people and governments for help for his beleaguered land. I was moved by his entreaties for help from any front. I was drawn to his genteel manner.

I felt I must do something to express my support. I decided to write to the ambassador. I penned a heartfelt letter, telling him that I prayed for the recovery of his country and the safety of his people. I provided him with my history, that I lived in the area, and that I was currently writing a book, and that perhaps I might interview the refugees and tell their stories.

After posting the letter to the ambassador, I thought little more about the correspondence although I continued to carefully analyze the political rhetoric spouted by world leaders. I watched with enormous sadness as refugees streamed out of Kuwait to tell their tales of horror. I worried about the people still trapped inside the small country. What was happening to them? I hoped that the world would not stand aside as it had done during massacres in Cambodia, a conflict and genocide that had so deeply affected my youth.

I called all many friends in the Middle East. I felt I had to do something, to help in some small way. Perhaps I could gather packets of goods and transport them to Egypt. I then reminded myself that the Kuwaiti government was very wealthy. They would take care of their citizens' basic needs. That's when my thoughts returned to a magazine story or a book. What the Kuwaitis needed was for the world to support them. Nothing is more powerful than war stories. That's when I made up my mind that I must return to the region and find the refugees, interview them and tell their stories. My decision was made, although I knew there would be many hurtles.

The Middle East was like my second home. I knew the culture. I had lived and worked in Riyadh, Saudi Arabia for many years, and knew that everything moves slower in the Middle East. I knew that I would require assistance in meeting the refugees. Although I had a number of friends who held prominent positions in the various Arab governments, none of them seemed "just right" to help me with the project.

Just as I was contemplating the momentous task ahead of me, the telephone rang. The ambassador from Kuwait was on the line. He was responding to my letter. I told him that I was surprised that he had taken the time to call. He asked me, "How could anyone fail to respond?" After a few moments spent discussing the situation, I spoke about my renewed determination to write a book based on interviews with the Kuwaiti refugees. I explained that it would be helpful to have a letter putting the minds of Kuwaitis at ease, that they were free to tell me their personal stories. I did not discuss the fact that most Arabs I know are tentative when talking publicly about their private lives. Their culture expects them to be demure, plus, most Arabs do not want to upset their governments.

The ambassador was interested in any plan that would alert the world to the current situation in his country. By the time our call ended, plans for made for me to fly to Washington the follow week to meet with the ambassador and his staff.

Other than what I had seen of him on the various television news shows, I knew nothing of Ambassador Al-Sabah. He did appear to be well-informed, well-mannered, and low-keyed. The Ambassador calmly related the facts, then rested his case, while the Iraqi ambassador, Mohammed Sadig Al-Mashat, insulted our intelligence by announcing that the Kuwaiti people wanted Iraq to rule their land, that they had asked for intervention from the Iraqi president to invade and put aside the Al-Sabah rulers.

I travelled to Washington as planned and obtained the letter introducing me as someone who wanted to hear the truth of what the refugees had experienced. (In my notes I relate details about meeting the ambassador, but since those memories are discussed in my Freedom Flight introduction following this Appendix, therefore I have not related those memories a second time.)

From Washington I traveled to London where I met Dr. Souad Al-Sabah, the wife of Abdullah Al-Mubarak, Al-Sabah, the only surviving son of Mubarak the Great. In Kuwait, Dr. Al-Sabah held a high position, for reasons related to her marriage as well as the fact Dr. Al-Sabah was a prominent Kuwaiti poet and writer. Dr. Al-Sabah and her children happened to be in London on the morning of the invasion, and they had remained there after the invasion and occupation. Dr. Sabah was working to help people like me get stories out about the Kuwaiti refugees. After learning that I was planning to dedicate the book to all the Kuwaitis killed during the invasion, with a special mention to the Emir's brother, Sheik Fahd Al-Sabah who was the royal who had been one of the first to die, Dr. Al-Sabah had a suggestion. She was kind enough to introduce me to Sheikher Fadila Al-Sabah, the Sheik's widow.

Meeting Sheikher Fadila and Dr. Al-Sabah was a night of sadness that I shall never forget. The Sheikher was extremely emotional. She appeared to love her husband very much and was in shock that he was dead. She was also uncertain as to the fate of her three sons, which created an extra dimension of fear and sadness.

From London I travelled on Cairo, Egypt, to meet with people who had recently escaped Kuwait through the deserts of Jordan, Iraq, and Saudi Arabia. Cairo was easy for me, as I was very familiar with Egypt after spending an enormous time over the years in Cairo with my ex-husband Peter Sasson, who was born and raised in Alexandria, Egypt. Peter's father was a European whose father owned many cotton plantations in Alexandria. Peter's mother was a Yugoslav who had met Peter's father in Northern Italy after World War II.

Peter and his wife Julie met me in Cairo. Peter had agreed to be the photographer for the book I was writing.

There were many refugees in Cairo, and all had tragic tales to share. Kuwait had been attacked unexpectedly, so no one was prepared. Many mothers had been separated from their children, some infants were misplaced in hospitals, while husbands and wives were lost to each other forever. The work in Cairo was a success.

From Cairo I travelled on to Riyadh, Saudi Arabia, the city that had been my home for twelve years, from 1978 through 1990.

While in Saudi Arabia, I visited embassy offices, makeshift schoolhouses, and hospitals, hearing tales of suffering, sorrow and helplessness. While in Riyadh, I asked the Kuwaiti Ambassador in Riyadh to provide me with the Kuwaiti government's telephone number in exile. The Kuwaiti royals had gathered in Taif. He did, and I called. I was surprised when the Minister of information answered the telephone. When I told him that I would like to fly to Taif and interview the Crown Prince and the Emir, he laughed and said, "Of course. We will send a private plane to Riyadh." He was serious. I laughed at the ease of it all, but telling him that it was not necessary, that I would book a flight from Riyadh to Taif. The following day I arrived in Taif, where I was greeted at the airport by one of the young Saudi royals. He said his name was Salem Al-Sabah and he wanted to be in the book I was writing. He was a charmer, a handsome young man, but I was on the way to see the Emir and the Crown Prince and my time was limited. It was clear that he was disappointed but he was so good natured that he laughed off his failure to be featured in the book.

(NOTE: Nearly fifteen years later when I dropped by the Kuwaiti Embassy in Washington, I asked to meet with the ambassador. I knew the ambassador's name, but I had never met him, as far as I knew. I was graciously escorted into the ambassador's office. He had a big smile on his face and asked me, "Do you remember me?" Unfortunately, I did not. Then he said, "I was your driver when you arrived in Taif. You were there to interview the Crown Prince and the Emir." I couldn't believe that young driver who was so pleasant and open was now Ambassador His Excellency Salem Abdullah Al-Jaber Al-Sabah. He had been appointed to Kuwait's most important ambassadorship and I had heard that the current ambassador was highly respected in his position. He was as down to earth as the first day I met him, chatting away, proudly showing me family photos. He wife was a beautiful Lebanese woman he had met while going to school in Beirut. He was the father of sons, and he said that he was trying to talk his wife into agreeing for him to buy a dog, a boxer. He was actually having nightly dreams of getting a boxer, he said. Of course, I was embarrassed not to have remembered him and had a moment of regret that I had not listened to his story on that long ago day in

1990 and written a chapter about him in my book, *The Rape of Kuwait*. Life is often filled with regrets, but we can't the past, so we move on.)

I was in Taif for only twenty-four hours. But it was plain that the Kuwaiti government was eager for a book to be written about the invasion and the human rights violations. Still, not one person asked me how the book was going, who was featured, if I had yet written any material, etc. I marveled at the differences between the Kuwaitis and the Saudis. The Kuwaitis were agreeable to letting the chips fall where they might. I would write a book according to what I discovered in my interviews. If the situation was reversed, and I was writing about the Saudis, they would demand to be in charge of my interviews, would insist upon a translator, would limit my questions, and would stop the proceedings if anyone was critical of the Saudi royal family. As time passed, I became more impressed with the openness of the Kuwaitis and of their royal family.

As promised, I was granted a lengthy interview with the Crown Prince and a much shorter meeting with the Emir. The Crown Prince appeared to be a very happy man, despite the current crisis. He flashed big smiles as he talked, relating all that had happened to him since the invasion.

The Emir was much more subdued and I felt he would prefer to be meeting with his ministers about the urgent matters at hand rather than speaking with a writer, although he was very courteous.

The Minister of Information politely invited me to stay in Taif for a few days, to become more familiar with the royals and the urgent tasks at hand. But I had a tight schedule, wanting to get back to London and then to Atlanta so that I might start writing the book. Therefore, I kept to my agenda, departing for Riyadh as planned.

After finishing up my final interviews in Riyadh, I made that planned detour to London where I met once again with Dr. Souad Al-Sabah. I was invited to her home, to a luxurious apartment near to Harrods Department store, where I met her very impressive children. It was easy to see that Dr. Sabah's children were her greatest joy. During one of our conversations, Dr. Al-Sabah told me about the biggest sorrow of her life, which was the loss of one of her sons. He struggled with asthma for his entire life. A year or so before, the family was departing Kuwait on a private plane when her son began having difficulties breathing. The poor boy was struggling for every breath. Everyone was distraught, pleading with the pilot to land as quickly as possible. But by the time they were back on the ground, Dr. Al-Sabah's beautiful and much loved son had drawn his last breath. Her son was dead.

I could feel her extreme sorrow and felt very badly for her loss, knowing from my own parents how wretched it is to lose a child.

*After returning to Atlanta, I started the writing process. Due to time constraints the book does read like a news report, but I was reassured that was the kind of book the public wanted. And so it was.

For additional information about Jean Sasson and her books, including maps, timelines, glossaries, and key facts about Saudi Arabia, please visit the author's website: http://www.JeanSasson.com
Blog: http://jeansasson.wordpress.com/
Facebook: http://www.facebook.com/AuthorJeanSasson
Twitter: http://twitter.com/jeansasson

NEW YORK TIMES BESTSELLING AUTHOR
JEAN SASSON

FOR THE LOVE
OF A SON

One Afghan woman's quest
for her stolen child

For the Love of a Son:
One Afghan woman's quest for her stolen child

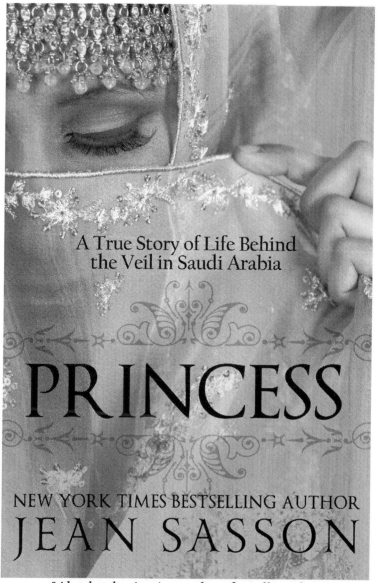

A True Story of Life Behind
the Veil in Saudi Arabia

PRINCESS

NEW YORK TIMES BESTSELLING AUTHOR
JEAN SASSON

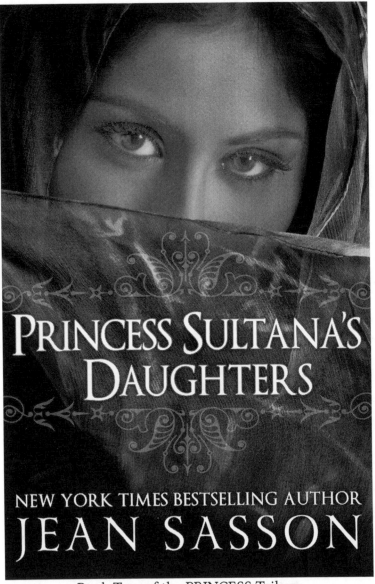

PRINCESS SULTANA'S DAUGHTERS

NEW YORK TIMES BESTSELLING AUTHOR

JEAN SASSON

Book Two of the PRINCESS Trilogy

Praise for PRINCESS: "A chilling story...a vivid account of
an air-conditioned nightmare..." —*Entertainment Weekly*

PRINCESS SULTANA'S CIRCLE

NEW YORK TIMES BESTSELLING AUTHOR
JEAN SASSON

Book Three of the PRINCESS trilogy

Praise for PRINCESS: "Shocking...candid...sad, sobering, and compassionate..." —*San Francisco Chronicle*

From the *New York Times*
bestselling author of
*Princess: A True Story
of Life Behind the Veil
in Saudi Arabia*

"Fascinating."
—*The Washington Post*

GROWING UP
BIN LADEN

OSAMA'S WIFE AND SON TAKE US
INSIDE THEIR SECRET WORLD

Najwa bin Laden | Omar bin Laden | Jean Sasson

"The most vivid look the American public has had at Bin
Laden's family life...The most complete account available."
—*New York Times*

"Fascinating." —*The Washington Post*

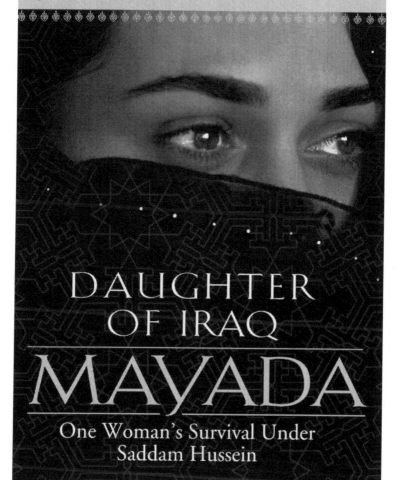

JEAN SASSON

DAUGHTER OF IRAQ

MAYADA

One Woman's Survival Under Saddam Hussein

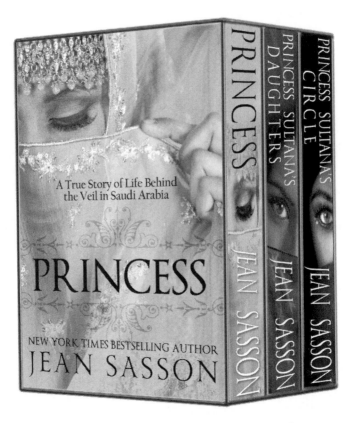

For the first time, the complete Princess Trilogy is available in one e-book!

"Fascinating...one is compelled to read just one more page, one more chapter once one has started this Arabian nightmare." —*Oxford Review*

"In this consistently gripping work, a Literary Guild alternate selection in cloth, the American-born Sasson recounts the life story of a Saudi princess she met while living in Saudi Arabia, offering a glimpse of the appalling conditions endured by even privileged women in the Middle East." —*Publisher's Weekly*

5115332R00138

Printed in Great Britain
by Amazon.co.uk, Ltd.,
Marston Gate.